T5-CCK-085

SPOTLIGHT *on*
High-Stakes Testing

FROM THE EDITORS OF THE
Harvard Education Letter

HARVARD EDUCATION PRESS

Library of Congress Control Number 2003106677
ISBN 1-891792-14-8

Published by Harvard Education Press,
an imprint of the Harvard Education Publishing Group

Harvard Education Press
8 Story Street
Cambridge, MA 02138

Cover Design: Anne Carter

The typefaces used in this book are Kuenstler 480 for text and Humanist 777 for display.

Contents

Introduction

When Education Is Put to the Test

Testing, teaching, and learning in the new high-stakes climate

By Michael Sadowski

Whether one sees on the horizon the threatening storm of "failing" schools or the dawning of a bright new day of accountability, one thing is certain: the forecast for public schools has changed dramatically with the passage of the 2001 No Child Left Behind Act. This legislation, with its key requirement that every public school in every state test every student in grades three through eight, may well be the most far-reaching federal education mandate in decades. The effects of this law are already being felt in schools, which in the fall of 2003 are being issued their first "report cards" indicating whether they are deemed in need of improvement. And, as states begin to implement their required curricular standards and testing plans over the next few years, there will be more and more assessments, more and more data, and more and more conclusions drawn about the condition of public education in the United States.

No Child Left Behind dramatically raises the ante on testing for educators, schools, and districts at a time when many states have already implemented tests that have serious consequences for students. In more than half the states around the country, students now cannot graduate from high school without having passed a state-level assessment. Promotion from grade to grade also depends on passing a standardized test in numerous states and municipalities. All of this adds up to a climate in which educational tests are now "high stakes" for a larger number of stakeholders than ever before.

The *Harvard Education Letter* has continuously monitored the growing high-stakes testing movement over the last several years, reporting on current research as it has been released and analyzing the likely effects of new state and federal regulations on the day-to-day work of teachers, administrators, and students. We therefore see it as both logical and urgent to introduce the Harvard Education Press's new Spotlight Series—a collection of books that will include reprints of classic HEL articles as well as new reports and commentaries on topics of critical interest to today's educators—with a volume on high-stakes testing.

The first section of this book, "Here To Stay? Making Testing Work," provides a variety of practical ideas for how educators and policymakers can make the most of what, for good or ill, is certain to be the most prominent feature of U.S. school reform for at least the next several years. In two related commentaries, noted UCLA researcher W. James Popham explains how accountability tests can and should be designed to serve students well and to provide the greatest possible boost to the quality of classroom instruction. *HEL*'s interview with Matthew Gandal, executive vice president of Achieve, Inc., brings these considerations down to the district level, highlighting how the Montgomery County, Md., Public Schools have designed district and school-level assessments and instruction that Gandal believes represent "model" alignment with state standards. Next, Judith A. Langer, a specialist in English/Language Arts instruction, discusses how teachers at individual schools can turn "accountability into opportunity." And Rebecca Wisniewski's teacher research feature brings strategies for the effective use of standardized test data directly into the classroom. Wisniewski shows how teachers can employ this data to inform instructional changes and meet the needs of individual learners.

In the next section, "The Larger Questions: Weighing the Costs and Benefits," authors consider some of the most fundamental issues that arise when we use tests to make high-stakes decisions about students and schools. In an updated version of my article from the September 2000 issue of *HEL*, "Are High-Stakes Tests Worth the Wager?" I revisit what happens when tests are used to make promotion or retention determinations about students, examining such potential unintended consequences as higher dropout rates, the narrowing of curriculum, and disproportionate effects on Latino and African American students. This piece is followed by two commentaries, one by veteran teacher, administrator, and teacher educator Marya R. Levenson, and the other by Jeff Howard, founder of the "efficacy" professional development model, who explore what's wrong and what's right with standardized tests.

Section three, "The Tests and the Curriculum," looks at aspects of schooling that can be affected in unexpected ways by the growing testing culture in schools. In "Collateral Damage," journalist and teacher Lisa Birk considers the fate of social-justice education—which many educators consider to be an invaluable curriculum for children and adolescents—in the context of state content standards and tests that do not often reflect an appreciation for this kind of learning. Next, writer and editor Jane Buchbinder examines what research says about the effects of arts education on student performance in the core subject areas (i.e., those that are the most widely tested)—and whether cultivating arts programs to raise test scores corrupts their purposes. Finally, education writer Karen Kelly ends the section with an exploration of how the fun of kindergarten is being lost in some elementary schools, which are focusing more and more heavily on raising children's test scores beginning in the earliest grades.

Two helpful appendices round out the volume. The first appendix presents some of the school accountability provisions that are central to the No Child Left Behind legislation. This excerpt from the U.S. Department of Education's "No Child Left Behind: A Desktop Reference" is a must-read for all educators who are required to abide by its regulations. It outlines what the law says about grade-level and subject-area testing requirements for schools, as well as the consequences for schools and districts that fail to demonstrate "adequate yearly progress" among all student subgroups.

The second appendix is a policy statement by the American Educational Research Association. It outlines what leaders of the foremost professional association for education researchers in the country agree are appropriate and inappropriate uses of high-stakes tests. These guidelines offer an essential yardstick by which to measure whether a state's or district's accountability system is fair, equitable, and consistent with what research has demonstrated are the most effective practices for improving student learning.

Graduation exams, grade-level promotion tests, school report cards, and other aspects of our increasingly high-stakes testing and accountability environment have both their proponents and their detractors. The proponents say such measures infuse a dose of much-needed scrutiny into a system that has become too lax, too damaged by low expectations, and too reliant on excuses to explain away what many see as deficiencies in the skills and knowledge of American children. The detractors argue that the tests drive curriculum in ways that are detrimental to student learning, peg too many students as failures, and distract policymakers and the public from such problems as poverty and racism, which they believe are the deepest causes of student underachievement. Evidence to support virtually all of these arguments—and many others—for and against high-stakes testing can be found in the pages that follow. We leave it up to the individual educator to make the best choices, based on the evidence, for her or his students.

Here to Stay?
Making Testing Work

Preparing for the Coming Avalanche of Accountability Tests

We can't get rid of high-stakes tests—but we can replace harmful ones with those that support both accountability and instruction

By W. James Popham

American educators will soon find themselves inundated by a profusion of state-level achievement tests spawned by the recently enacted No Child Left Behind Act. Signed into law by President Bush in January 2002, this significant new federal statute calls for a dramatic expansion of state-level achievement testing in math and reading in grades 3–8. Such increased assessment, if appropriate, could help our nation's children learn what they ought to be learning. It is more likely, however, that this enlargement of statewide achievement testing will only heighten the harmful effects that most of today's state-level achievement tests are having on children.

Whether the new, federally mandated achievement tests turn out to have a positive or negative impact on students will depend almost totally on the types of tests that educational decisionmakers choose to install. If traditionally constructed achievement tests are used—tests akin to those now widely employed—then we will surely witness a continued test-triggered erosion of educational quality. In contrast, if more suitable state-level achievement tests are installed, then their impact on instruction could be quite positive.

It is absolutely urgent, therefore, that all relevant stakeholders immediately let their state's educational leaders know that the new achievement tests should be designed so that they have a positive impact on schooling. And, because the new tests must be up and running by the 2005–06 school year, state education officials must soon get cracking on building assessments to satisfy the new law's requirements. Will state policy makers opt for the "same-old, same-old" achievement tests, or will tests be chosen that truly support instruction?

HARMFUL TESTS

Currently, statewide achievement tests are administered annually in almost every state, typically at several grade levels. Students' performances on these tests often play a prominent role in evaluating the effectiveness of educators at both the district and school levels. Newspaper rankings of school-by-school scores on these achievement tests, for example, are used by citizens to determine which schools are wonderful and which are woeful.

Moreover, in many states student test performance can also have serious consequences for individual students (such as the denial of a high school diploma or grade-to-grade retention). It should be apparent, then, that statewide achievement tests are important assessment instruments. Is it any wonder that such assessments are often referred to as "high-stakes tests"? Yet, these high-stakes assessment instruments are typically having a decisively negative impact on the quality of schooling provided to a state's students.

First, there is rampant curricular reductionism wherein teachers tend to reduce the instructional attention they give to any skills or knowledge not assessed on a statewide achievement test. Curricular content not addressed on a statewide test is apt to get short shrift in classrooms.

Because of pressure to boost their students' scores on high-stakes tests, many teachers steer clear of any content that's not likely to boost scores. Yet, a student who gets shortchanged on content is a miseducated student. Today's state-level achievement tests are triggering the kind of curricular construction that miseducates massive numbers of our nation's children.

A second harmful consequence of today's statewide accountability tests is that they foster excessive test-focused drilling. Many teachers these days are being pushed so hard to raise their students' scores that their classrooms have been transformed into drill-dominated, test-preparation factories.

Most teachers, of course, are familiar with the research evidence showing that, if teachers provide their students with ample "time-on-task" practice (on tasks similar to those found on a test), students' scores will rise. There is, however, no evidence to support the instructional payoff of "eternity-on-task"! And that's what many students feel they've been put through after enduring seemingly endless hours of test-preparation drills. Such drilling can stamp out the joy that students ought to be deriving from learning. Education can be, and often should be, genuinely exciting. But the only excitement in a drill-dominated classroom takes place when the end-of-period buzzer goes off.

Finally, a third harmful impact of today's statewide accountability tests is that they often lead to two forms of outright dishonesty on the part of teachers who are pressured by account-ability measures. Some teachers—thankfully not all that many yet—seriously bend test-administration rules so that their students will score better. Some give students more time to complete the test than they're supposed to. Others roam the classroom giving students on-the-spot suggestions to "rethink" incorrect answers. Even more blatantly, some teachers have actually been apprehended giving students a list of correct an-swers before administering a high-stakes test. If we truly want our teachers to function *in loco parentis*, how can we permit these proxy parents to model dishonesty for our children?

Equally serious is the sort of unethical test preparation that some teachers provide to their students before the administra-tion of a statewide achievement test. Students are provided with practice items that are nearly identical (or, in some cases, *are* identical) to the actual items on the test. Then, later, when students take the actual test and encounter such already prac-ticed items, they realize that they have been made unwilling conspirators in a teacher-contrived fraud. After such an experi-ence, how will students regard their teachers in the future? Dis-honesty breeds dishonesty, on either side of the teacher's desk.

In sum, statewide accountability tests, although often in-stalled with the best of intentions, are having at least the three negative consequences identified here, namely, curricular re-ductionism, excessive test-focused drilling, and the modeling of dishonesty. Clearly, such tests are harming, not helping, educa-tion.

But statewide accountability tests are not going to go away. Indeed, even if the No Child Left Behind Act had never made it to the president's desk, there would still be accountability tests almost everywhere in the U.S. And that's because our nation's citizens, and the policymakers who represent them, have lost confidence in our public schools. The only way this widespread erosion in public confidence in schools can be turned around is with evidence—lots of it—that U.S. schools are truly worth the tax dollars we pour into them.

We do not have statewide accountability tests because educators yearned for them. On the contrary, such tests were installed by skeptical policymakers who, often over heated protests from the education profession, wanted proof that our public schools were working. Today, therefore, no amount of rhetoric from educators, however persuasive, will satisfy the demand for test-based evidence that our schools are successful. All this would be true even without a new federal law calling for the marked expansion of statewide achievement testing.

Anyone arguing for the abolition of high-stakes accountability tests might as well be whistling into a hurricane. Statewide accountability tests—in ever greater numbers—are here to stay.

WHAT'S TO BE DONE?

That sounds like a pretty gloomy prophecy. But there's a solution strategy that we can employ. We simply need to use more appropriate state-level achievement tests. The reason that we see today's state-level tests having such an adverse impact on American education is that those tests are not suitable for the evaluation of educational quality. And yet, of course, the evaluation of educational quality is the cornerstone of any state-level accountability system.

Today's achievement tests have been constructed according to a traditional measurement model that's focused on providing comparative interpretations of examinees' test performance. In order to yield meaningful comparisons of student test performance—to show, for example, that Student A scored in the 60th percentile, Student B in the 65th—a traditional test's items need to do a super job of spreading out students' scores. Many of the items on today's state-level achievement tests are linked directly to students' socioeconomic status or to inherited academic aptitudes. These items do a good job in spreading out students' scores, but they also assess what students bring to school, not what they learn there.

Traditional achievement tests do have an important function, namely, to allow both teachers and parents to see how a student's performance compares to that of other students in a normative group. That's useful information. But such comparative information is not suitable for the evaluation of schools.

Statewide achievement tests need not be built according to a traditional, comparison-focused measurement model. It is possible to create instructionally supportive accountability tests that not only supply accurate, credible evidence regarding the educational effectiveness of our schools, but also help teachers do a better job of instructing their students.

The nature of such dual-purpose tests is described in a pair of reports issued by the independent Commission on Instructionally Supportive Assessment. The reports make clear that state-level, high-stakes achievement tests can be constructed so that they provide solid accountability evidence, yet are also instructionally supportive. (See the following chapter for more on "instructionally sensitive" tests.)

In the coming months, when state-level decisionmakers are determining how best to satisfy the brand new federal assessment requirements, we have a marvelous opportunity to modify outmoded measurement approaches and to turn instead to the creation of statewide achievement tests that can benefit our students.

If it turns out that tomorrow's avalanche of statewide achievement tests are the same as today's, then we will surely have muffed it.

This commentary originally appeared in the Harvard Education Letter's *May/June 2002 issue. It has been edited for this volume.*

FOR FURTHER INFORMATION

Commission on Instructionally Supportive Assessment. "Building Tests to Support Instruction and Accountability: A Guide for Policymakers." Available online at www.aasa.org/issues_and_insights/assessment/Building_Tests.pdf

W.J. Popham. *Classroom Assessment: What Teachers Need to Know* (3rd ed.). Boston: Allyn & Bacon, 2002.

W.J. Popham. *Modern Educational Measurement: Practical Guidelines for Educational Leaders* (3rd ed.). Boston: Allyn & Bacon, 2000.

W.J. Popham. *Testing! Testing! What Every Parent Should Know About School Tests*. Boston: Allyn & Bacon, 2000.

W.J. Popham. *The Truth About Testing: An Educator's Call to Action*. Arlington, Va.: Association for Supervision and Curriculum Development, 2001.

Are Your State's Tests Instructionally Sensitive?

High-quality assessments share three key attributes

By W. James Popham

The No Child Left Behind Act (NCLB) has imposed the need for a state's educators to promote substantial annual improvements in students' scores on state-determined NCLB achievement tests. Where these improvements do not occur, deficient schools and/or districts will be identified as having failed to achieve adequate yearly progress (AYP). After two consecutive years of AYP failure, schools or districts receiving federal NCLB funds will be placed on an improvement track linked to increasingly severe sanctions.

If a state's education decisionmakers have chosen to install *instructionally insensitive* NCLB tests—that is, tests incapable of detecting improvements in teachers' instructional activities—then the undergirding rationale for test-based AYP obviously becomes senseless. How can educators be expected to promote students' substantial improvement on tests that are essentially unable to gauge the impact of either good or bad teaching?

Instructionally insensitive tests, therefore, will almost certainly lead to the inaccurate evaluation of a state's schools and districts. And, just as surely, such tests will subvert the praiseworthy educational aspirations of the congressional lawmakers who crafted NCLB. These tests will certainly cause rampant labeling of a state's educators as ineffectual. But what if those labels are wrong?

If *instructionally sensitive* NCLB tests are in place, however, then a state's teachers will be able to design and deliver the best instruction of which they are capable. High-quality instruction will lead to higher scores, and effective teaching will be identified and then applauded. Ineffective instruction will also be identified so that it can be improved.

Instructionally sensitive state-level NCLB achievement tests must possess three attributes. First, the skills and/or bodies of knowledge the tests assess must be adequately described so that teachers have a clear idea of what their students must master. Second, the assessed skills and/or bodies of knowledge must be sufficiently small in number so that teachers are not overwhelmed by too many assessment targets. Third, the tests' results must permit teachers to identify whether a student has mastered each assessed skill and/or body of knowledge.

CLEAR DESCRIPTIONS OF ASSESSMENT TARGETS

Today's statewide achievement tests are typically supposed to assess, at least in some general fashion, a state's content standards (i.e., the skills and knowledge designated as state-approved curricular aims). But in many states, those content standards are ambiguous. In fact, a number of states have chosen to make their content standards nothing more than general labels like "algebraic understandings." Such designations are intended to describe a bevy of more specific curricular outcomes referred to as "benchmarks," "performance indicators," and the like.

One straightforward way to determine whether a state test's assessment targets are well described is to assemble a small group of teachers, perhaps a half-dozen or so, then find out to what extent they independently concur in their interpretation of the nature of any assessment target. After providing the group with whatever descriptive materials are available, they should then be asked to write, in their own words, what the meaning is of a set of randomly selected benchmarks. After the teachers have independently written their descriptions, those descriptions should be compared to determine how similar they are. The more alike the teachers' independently created descriptors are, the more confidence one can have in the clarity of descriptions regarding the assessed skills and knowledge. If the teacher-generated descriptions are not homogeneous, this lack of clarity may serve as evidence of a test's instructional insensitivity. If, because of inadequate descriptions of what's to be measured by a state's NCLB tests, the tests turn out to measure one set of skills and knowledge but the state's teachers aim their instruction at another, then students' test performances will surely not indicate how well their teachers have been teaching.

A MANAGEABLE NUMBER OF ASSESSMENT TARGETS

Too many targets can overwhelm. That's true with hunters; that's true with teachers. If an NCLB test contends that it measures 30 or 40 curricular targets, teachers will be unable to focus their instructional plans properly. An NCLB test that purports to measure too many content standards is certain to be instructionally insensitive.

In the first place, because there is a limited amount of time to administer an achievement test, especially to young students, it is patently impossible to measure children's mastery of large numbers of curricular aims. That's because it is typically impossible to measure a student's mastery of a particular curricular aim with only one or two test items. And if there are numerous curricular aims to be assessed, you can be sure that the test simply cannot measure all of them *well*—or even measure some of them *at all*. Thus, what's going to be assessed on each year's NCLB test frequently turns into a guessing game— a game in which teachers often guess wrong. It is difficult for teachers to focus their classroom instruction accurately if they are forced to conjecture about what's to be assessed.

Typically, of course, NCLB tests are based on a state-approved curriculum that frequently contains an excessive number of content standards or benchmarks. Thus, the underlying reason that NCLB tests attempt to measure too many curricular targets is often the state's curriculum itself. Nonetheless, a state NCLB test that asserts that it will assess a large number of curricular targets has, by its acquiescence to the state's too-numerous targets, presented the state's teachers with an onerous and unhelpful set of assessment objectives.

One way to determine whether a state's tests have too many assessment targets is simply to count those targets. There may be no "magic maximum number" of assessment targets for an NCLB test, but sensible people can typically recognize too many targets when they see them. For instance, if you learned that the 5th-grade NCLB tests in your state supposedly measure students' mastery of 14 reading benchmarks and 33 mathematics benchmarks, you'd have little difficulty in concluding that too many assessment targets were being measured. For a

5th-grade teacher to focus sensibly on 47 assessment targets in reading and math (not to mention the teacher's need to deal with curricular aims in other subject areas) is impossible. In some states, NCLB tests are being used that require teachers at a given grade level to focus their instructional attention on a hundred or more math and reading benchmarks. This just can't be done.

INSTRUCTIONALLY INFORMATIVE RESULTS

If NCLB tests do not give teachers their students' results in a form that permits them to determine which segments of their instruction have been effective or ineffective, those tests will be instructionally insensitive. Teachers cannot use such test results to improve the quality of their instruction. Over the long haul, students won't be taught better because teachers won't know which parts of their instruction need improvement.

If the tests are organized around a modest number of assessment targets, say six or seven, then the tests' results should be reported in such a way that a teacher can determine which of the targets were mastered (by the teacher's students) and which weren't. If teachers don't know which parts of their instruction have been working, they won't be able to improve.

To find out whether an NCLB test's reporting structure is satisfactory, it makes sense once more to talk to teachers who have been on the receiving end of the reports. When teachers look at test results, they should be able to spell out exactly how a set of test results will help them, if at all, in judging the caliber of particular segments of their teaching. NCLB tests that fail to provide meaningful per-standard or per-benchmark feedback to teachers are instructionally insensitive.

IS INSTRUCTIONAL SENSITIVITY SUFFICIENT?

Instructional sensitivity is an important first step toward ensuring that testing programs fulfill the stated goals of the NCLB legislation. But an NCLB test can be instructionally sensitive yet not benefit a state's students. Here's why: Instructionally sensitive tests can be built to assess *low-aspiration* curricular aims. An instructionally sensitive test could satisfy all three attributes I've just described, yet deal with truly trifling curricular outcomes. Putting it another way, instructional sensitivity is simply not enough.

Disturbingly, to avoid the appearance that too many state educators will appear to be ineffective, officials in some states have decided to have their state's NCLB tests assess skills and knowledge that are not genuinely challenging (or they have set their "proficiency" levels much lower than will be good for the state's children). Such actions may lead to fewer identifications of failing schools, but serious educational harm will be done to the state's children by trivializing the state's assessment aspirations.

In short, NCLB tests need to measure significant skills and knowledge that children ought to be mastering. If a state's tests assess students' mastery of only low-level curricular outcomes, then all the instructional sensitivity in the world won't make those tests contribute to children's well-being.

A longer version of this commentary was prepared for the National School Boards Association in February 2003.

Lessons of a "Model" Program

Aligning district tests and curricula with state requirements

An interview with Matthew Gandal

Under the No Child Left Behind Act, school districts all over the country will be required to show student gains on new state-level assessments, or they will risk being designated as in need of improvement. In an effort to raise the achievement of all its students on the new, more rigorous Maryland state tests, officials of the Montgomery County Public Schools developed a grade-by-grade set of curriculum frameworks and assessments and contracted with Achieve, Inc., an independent nonprofit organization, to evaluate their effectiveness. Achieve, which normally assesses accountability systems at the state level for "quality and coherence," praised the Montgomery County assessments as rigorous, high-quality measures that are good predictors of students' performance on state-level tests. Achieve also indicated that, with some minor revisions, the district's curriculum frameworks "can be on a par with the best in the nation and the world." In Spring 2003, HEL spoke with Achieve executive vice president Matthew Gandal about the lessons educators from other districts can learn from the work in Montgomery County.*

HEL: A recent story in *Education Week* characterized the Montgomery County, Maryland, standards and assessment work as a "model." Would this be an accurate assessment? If so, why?

Gandal: Yes, I think it's accurate. In standards-based reform, much of the attention has been on states as the entities responsible for setting academic standards, developing testing systems to measure the standards, and then putting accountability systems in place based on those standards. What we found in Montgomery County is that there's an equally important role for school districts around that same set of issues—not competing with the state or duplicating what the state's done, but instead creating a complementary set of assessments and instructional materials that are aligned with state goals and the state exams.

Maryland will have a new set of graduation exams that count over the next few years. They've really raised the bar. Kids will have to pass a set of end-of-course tests to graduate. In the past they only had to pass a very low-level, 8th-grade kind of basic competency test. What Montgomery County has done is create semester exams in those same courses, the goal being to give feedback earlier in the year to the kids, the parents, and the teachers about how those kids are doing so that something can be done about it before they take that end-of-year test. They wanted to know whether doing well on these local semester exams would put their students on a path to succeed on the state exams at the end of the year. In this case, the answer was yes.

Then they asked us to look at the curriculum frameworks that drive the instructional materials in the county. How well aligned are these to the state standards? That's one set of questions that we think districts ought to be asking more often. It all sounds sort of logical, but it doesn't look to us like it's happening in enough places yet.

The antithesis to doing it this way would be a district saying, "We want our own assessments, so we're going to use the Iowa Test of Basic Skills or the Stanford 10 [2003] as a district test. Then we're going to have students take the state exams at the end of the year." Essentially you have two competing exams given at the same time of year, not aligned with one another. Unfortunately, that seems to happen more often than the model we're seeing play out in Montgomery County.

HEL: Why do districts use exams like the Iowa Test that are not aligned with state frameworks or exams?

Gandal: Well, it's faster, it's cheaper, and it's a known quantity. People think they understand what these exams mean and what they measure. They've used them before, and they're somewhat familiar. They're clearly easier to get hold of and put in place. Montgomery County developed its own semester exams—not an easy thing to do. A lot of school districts don't have the capacity to do that. We've heard states and districts talk a lot about the need for these sorts of diagnostic assessments. They recognize that it's not enough just to have an end-of-grade test, but we haven't yet seen very many models of how to get it done. Clearly it requires expertise and resources beyond what some districts probably have.

HEL: What about those systems that can't afford to develop their own assessments? What can they do?

Gandal: Well, that's where I think the states need to somehow lend a helping hand. Until recently districts didn't want other people meddling in this area. I think just recently you're finding that districts are saying, "We need help. The standards aren't enough; the assessments aren't enough." So the states are trying to figure out what to do about it. But ideally the states would help districts put rigorous curricula in place. They'd create models, they'd adapt ones that exist somewhere else, they'd help a group of districts in a state work together and pool resources.

One thing we have in mind with a group of states that are working together to raise math standards is to see if we can get some of the districts to work together and possibly share things they've already created. Or, again, to pool resources to create, for example, diagnostic tests for various grades, then share and use them together. It's about pooling resources, talent, and expertise rather than having each district figure this out on its own.

HEL: What does Achieve look for in a good set of curriculum frameworks and a good set of assessments?

Gandal: The standards need to be clear and understandable. They need to be articulated in such a way that both teachers and parents can understand them and arrive at a common interpretation. They can't be vague. They can't be general. They have to be fairly explicit in terms of what content and skills are expected in each grade. On the other hand, they can't just be laundry lists that stuff everything in they can possibly fit. They have to be focused and manageable.

They also have to clearly progress from grade to grade, rather than repeat the same concepts over and over again with no progression. They need to be rigorous, but reasonable. To know how rigorous is rigorous enough, we look at what other states expect, what some of the higher-achieving states or countries expect of their kids. If one state is expecting students to master what counts for Algebra I by the end of 8th grade and another state doesn't require that until 9th or 10th grade, that's significant.

When it comes to tests, the basic question we're trying to answer is, if you have good standards, how well do your tests measure them? There are several sides to this. First, we want to make sure that everything on the test can be found in the standards. It's sort of a basic fairness issue: Are you only testing what you're telling the teachers and students they need to learn? Also, how well are you measuring the most important concepts and skills in your standards? There's great variation in that. In a lot of places we found that tests are much better at measuring the lower-level skills and not very good at measuring the higher-level skills. They're lopsided; they don't adequately measure the depth and breadth of the academic standards.

And, ultimately, we try to get a sense of how rigorous exams are. How challenging are the questions, and to what extent is the difficulty related to the content or the skills embedded in them, rather than to tricks built into the questions that have more to do with learning how to take a test than really knowing something? There's a whole series of steps we go through to uncover all that.

HEL: How specifically have the new federal requirements under the No Child Left Behind Act affected this work? What is particularly important for school districts to be thinking about now?

Gandal: Clearly, No Child Left Behind (NCLB) has upped the ante on all this for states and districts. There may have been some hard-charging states that were putting very comprehensive testing and accountability systems in place, but NCLB all of a sudden required them all to do it and had a pretty strict set of rules you needed to follow while you were doing it. That's a new environment for the states and districts, and it's frankly a new environment for Achieve to be working in.

All of a sudden the states have to create a lot more tests. They have to have them grade by grade, not just at some grades. We're trying to help states maintain the quality of their tests as they're frantically trying to purchase or build new ones, and to make sure that the tests are really well aligned with standards and don't shortcut that. It brings you right back to the question I mentioned earlier: Are they going to take the easy route and try to take standardized tests that already exist and put them in the grades where they don't have them, or are they going to pay more attention to quality and alignment and vertical articulation of their tests? This is a very big challenge the states are facing.

Another effect of NCLB is that there are going to be a lot more "low-performing schools" [by federal standards] because the bar is being raised. We think it's pretty important that states have strategies for helping those schools. We're not sure what the strategies are yet. We haven't seen a lot of dialogue on this. But people are going to be asking, what's the solution? What are we going to do with these schools? It's not enough just to have a list. This is hard stuff, particularly at a time when the economy is in a downturn. So, what tough choices are states going to have to make about resources? And what's the role of the school district in this? We think we'll probably be pretty busy trying to help states work through these things, and trying to keep a focus on quality while they're worrying about compliance.

HEL: If you were to sum up, what lessons do you think those designing standards and assessments at the district level can take from the Montgomery County example?

Gandal: *Lesson 1:* Pay close attention to the state standards. Don't try to compete with the state; instead, try to align with and possibly exceed the state standards.

Lesson 2: Compare what you're doing with what others are doing beyond your state. It can only help to improve the quality of what you're putting in place if you look at the best examples around you.

Lesson 3: There's got to be an actual concrete curriculum in place that aligns with the state standards. Having no curriculum or total flexibility on curriculum is probably not the best solution.

Lesson 4: End-of-year assessments are necessary but not sufficient. There have to be more regular ways to diagnose how well students are doing. Assessments don't have to be as large scale and as formal as the kind that come at the end of the year; they can be much more teacher driven and applied. But assessment has to be a year-round activity aligned with the curriculum, and Montgomery County is showing in part how that can be done.

This interview originally appeared in the Harvard Education Letter's *July/ August 2003 issue.*

FOR FURTHER INFORMATION

Achieve, Inc. *Measuring Up: A Report on Education Standards and Assessments for Montgomery County.* Washington, D.C.: Achieve, 2003. Available online at www.achieve.org/dstore.nsf/lookup/montgomery/$file/ montgomery.pdf

D.J. Hoff, "Maryland's District Curriculum Cited as Model." *Education Week,* February 26. 2003. Available online at www.edweek.com/ew/ew_pri ntstory.cfm?slug=24achieve.h22

U.S. Department of Education. "No Child Left Behind: A Desktop Reference." Washington, D.C.: Author, 2002. Available online at www.ed.gov/offices/OESE/reference

Turning Accountability into Opportunity

How thoughtful, well-connected learning can get stifled—and what to do about it

By Judith A. Langer

Administrators and teachers across the country are trying hard to help their students learn more and score higher on high-stakes tests. But why are some schools and districts achieving much more than others? This question was the focus of a series of research projects conducted over a five-year period by the National Research Center on English Learning and Achievement (CELA). The studies focused on teachers' professional lives, state and district policy, and reading and writing instruction.

The CELA studies have found that more successful schools and districts have coherent programs that offer students connected, thought-provoking learning experiences at all grade levels. This, of course, merely reaffirms what most educators already know. Perhaps more importantly, however, the studies also highlight the three behaviors or attitudes that present the biggest obstacles to making this learning model a reality.

TEACHING TO TESTS

An obstacle emerges in schools and districts where test for-
mats and test answers become ends unto themselves. On the
other hand, where educators use high-stakes tests and the standards-based movement to reach greater goals, student learning
is enhanced. Here, test preparation becomes an opportunity for
professional collaboration, inquiry, and growth, as teachers and
administrators work together to ensure that students do not
merely perform well on the tests but also in their schoolwork
and their lives. One way teachers and administrators can help
make this happen is to take the tests themselves with an eye
toward understanding the underlying knowledge or skills that
will "pay off," not only in good test performance but also in situations beyond the test.

In one state where students were required to do persuasive
writing on their 11th-grade test, two groups of schools followed
very different approaches. One group's administrators mandated that persuasive writing be assigned and practiced for much
of the students' junior year. Teachers duplicated old test assignments and developed or purchased new prompts that followed
the wording and format of the test. Teachers in another group
of schools focused on students learning the various purposes
for writing—including but not limited to persuasion—and the
ways in which those purposes affect organization, syntax, and
word choice.

During the first few years, students in both groups of schools
benefited from preparation, but those in the second group
scored somewhat higher. In the fourth year, the state changed
the testing prompt, and students were asked to do a different
type of writing. The first group's scores plummeted, while the
other's remained high. The students whose teachers focused
on the concept of purpose in writing, not just on test prepara-

tion, were better prepared to understand and meet the demands of newly encountered writing tasks.

USING NARROW DEFINITIONS OF LEARNING

Another obstacle is the tendency to overemphasize "the right answer." When teachers treat answers as the primary or even sole evidence of learning, lessons end once students have given these answers. Students become conditioned to guess what the teacher wants, and even when they get an answer right they aren't sure why. On the other hand, student learning is enhanced when deeper learning of concepts is the goal. Students have the opportunity to grapple with what they are studying— together, alone, on email, in the library—and reach a deeper and more connected understanding of new ideas. In the higher performing schools in our studies, even the lowest performing students are taught to think and discuss and write about new ideas in ways that clarify their understanding and make them better learners.

In CELA, we've called this a focus on "generative learning." As a matter of course, students are expected to go beyond giving definitions and learn to explain, analyze, critique, research, and interpret. The following example illustrates the concept of generative learning in practice.

After one middle-school class read Karen Cushman's *The Midwife's Apprentice*, the teacher assessed students' understanding of the novel through class discussions and writing assignments about the book's content, theme, and style. Next, she asked the students to research the life and social patterns of the Renaissance. They gave oral and written reports comparing what they had learned with the conditions depicted in *The Midwife's Apprentice* and analyzed how the novel's plot reflected the times. Students then worked in groups to answer questions such as "How did the title character's social environment affect her?" and "How might her life be different if she lived in our time?" Later they chose among several other stories to examine how characters' roles are often a function of their times and to identify some features that transcend time. Using this generative approach, students learned to make connections among such seemingly disparate elements as literature, history, and contemporary life.

VIEWING DIVERSITY AS A PROBLEM

A third obstacle is the attitude among some teachers that student diversity—whether personal, cultural, physical, or experiential—is a hindrance to effective teaching and learning. Student learning is actually enhanced when teachers consider diversity an intellectually interesting opportunity and use it as a way to enrich the classroom experience. Students hear a variety of perspectives and learn to weigh other points of view while rethinking their own ideas, interpretations, and ways of doing things. This involves embracing and building on the variety of cultural and experiential differences that all students bring to their learning.

In higher performing schools, homogeneity is seen as a disadvantage, as setting limits to what students will discuss and think about. Teachers in higher performing schools try to help their students see diversity in their own backgrounds, interests, and histories, and to use diverse perspectives to their own and others' advantage, even in classes where the students seem to be very similar. They help their students look beyond as well as within their classrooms, cultures, and generations to enrich their knowledge about the topics at hand.

For example, one middle-grade classroom we studied included two students with profound hearing loss who contributed to class discussions through a sign-language interpreter. These students brought unique and important perspectives to the class. They tested their classmates' preconceptions—and had their own ideas challenged as well.

In another classroom, this one composed largely of English-language learners from a variety of countries, high school students were asked to choose stories from home (fictional or retold from real life) and to write them, preserving the original linguistic structure as closely as possible. These stories were used as a way to help the students focus on content, language, and structure. Their teacher encouraged them to look for similarities and differences among the stories and used these as points of discussion.

Overall, these studies indicate that effective learning occurs in schools where close attention is paid to what gets taught and how, and where teachers have opportunities to collaborate on effective strategies. Proactive schools can turn the seemingly restrictive standards-based movement into an opportunity to advance effective learning.

This chapter originally appeared in the Harvard Education Letter's *March/ April 2001 issue under the title "Turning Obstacles into Opportunity." It has been edited for this volume.*

Making the Most of Standardized Test Data

How teacher research can inform instructional change

By Rebecca Wisniewski

THE CONTEXT

The Charlotte M. Murkland School in Lowell, Massachusetts, is an inner-city school with approximately 530 students in preschool through 4th grade. The school is located in the section of the city known as The Acre, which has historically been where new immigrants to the city settle. The Murkland has a Khmer bilingual strand, and an estimated 60 percent of our students come from non-English-speaking homes. Our poverty rate is one of the highest in the city, about 84 percent.

The school was built ten years ago, and the faculties from two schools joined to form our teaching staff, which has a commitment to providing the best instruction possible to all students. The Murkland is challenged with a host of problems that can only truly be understood if you are there. Still, year after year teachers remain. Perhaps most telling is that we do not have difficulty getting substitute teachers to come to the building. We like to think of ourselves as a large family.

The Massachusetts Comprehensive Assessment System (MCAS) test is a fact of life for all public school children in Massachusetts. If the students who sit in front of me today do not pass this test in high school, they will not receive a diploma. They will not be able to attend any public college in the state. This one test acts, in many ways, as gatekeeper to mainstream America. Although many professional educators feel that the test would serve the public better and would be less discriminatory if it were part of a formula that included other criteria such student grades, it is a reality we must deal with.

My personal action research with the MCAS began three years ago when my colleagues and I were troubled by the results of the 2000 test. Murkland teachers have always made every effort to provide all students with a solid education. I felt that surely embedded somewhere in the school's MCAS score report would be indications of this effort, as well as clues to how we could better address our students' needs.

RESEARCH QUESTIONS

1. What do our MCAS scores tell us about our curriculum? Are there curriculum segments that are working especially well? If so, what are they and how can we build on them? To what curriculum areas do we need to pay special attention?

2. How are certain student subgroups, particularly our English-language learners, doing in relation to the general district population?

3. Given the high stakes associated with the MCAS test, what can we as a staff do to prepare our students better?

METHODS

The MCAS School Report contains a great deal of data that can be extrapolated and used to inform instruction. Some of the results are reported in graphs, but much of the data is presented in large tables that often obscure whatever conclusions one might be able to draw from them. By simply graphing some of this tabular data, it became more meaningful to the school staff and allowed for easier comparison of subgroup scores. I felt that if my colleagues viewed the results in this way, the good as well as the bad, they would think about their own teaching practices. Good teachers adjust their practices every year. This data would provide solid evidence on which to base these changes.

Our team presented the MCAS results graphically to the Murkland School staff after inputting the data into Microsoft Excel. The first set of graphs we generated showed how different subgroups performed in comparison to the school as a whole. Next, I calculated what percentage of available points students earned on different sections of the test and compared them. I hoped that this information would help us to target specific areas of our curriculum. Teachers viewed the Excel graphs before school, during common planning times, or at staff meetings. The information stimulated discussions about what might have led to improvements. Conversely, it also sparked conversations about why one particular group had not done as well as it might have on a specific section of the test. Out of these discussions, we developed an action plan for the following year that unified our efforts and expectations.

FINDINGS

Our analysis of the 2000 MCAS scores uncovered a number of positive results that buoyed our spirits. Our school had smaller percentages of students with disabilities and limited English proficient students who failed the test than the district as a whole. These findings validated our teachers' efforts with these at-risk student subgroups.

MCAS test scores are normally reported in the following scaled score intervals: "warning," "needs improvement," "proficient," and "advanced." By taking the extra step of observing where individual students fell within these intervals, it became apparent that more than half who were in the warning category needed only between one and four additional points to reach the next interval and pass.

Other findings suggested ways we could refocus aspects of our curriculum. In analyzing our 4th-grade English/Language Arts (ELA) scores, we found to our surprise that Murkland students' performance was closer to state and district averages on "standard English conventions" than it was on "topic development." Put simply, students were better at punctuation and capitalization than they were at telling a story.

From our data the following year, it was also clear that students were not doing well on the test's open-response questions (see Fig. 1). The number of points that each student scored on each open-response question was determined using the MCAS item analysis report. In graphing this information, we noted that 16 percent of our students did not even attempt to answer the questions, and about half scored only one or two points out of a possible four.

In looking at other data across several years, we noticed a trend involving our students' Developmental Reading Assessment (DRA) scores. The DRA test requires that students read a passage aloud while the teacher takes a running record of their decoding. Next, the student must retell the story, thereby demonstrating comprehension. Every grade showed improvement in reading, but the rate of improvement appeared to flatten out as students reached 3rd and 4th grade. To get a clearer sense of why this was happening, I isolated the test scores for students who did not improve in one 3rd-grade class. In this sample

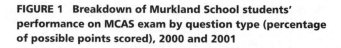

FIGURE 1 Breakdown of Murkland School students' performance on MCAS exam by question type (percentage of possible points scored), 2000 and 2001

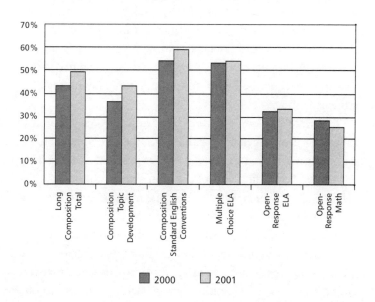

study, I noticed that students were not going to the next DRA level due to a lack of comprehension. It seemed that their ability to decode exceeded their ability to comprehend.

HOW THE RESEARCH HAS AFFECTED PRACTICE

To address our students' apparent weakness in the area of topic development, the faculty expanded writing instruction and decided to have the Title I resource teacher work with the entire 4th grade. Students were taught to use new graphic organizers to plan their writing and generate details. This led to the development of a writing conference sheet based on the MCAS writing rubric, which teachers used as a basis from which to discuss with students the strengths and weaknesses in their compositions. A schoolwide effort to teach paragraphing early in the year became another priority. Finally, 3rd-grade faculty joined the effort by dovetailing their writing instruction with that of the 4th grade teachers. Our comparison of 2000 and 2001 MCAS results clearly showed that these combined efforts had an impact on the MCAS results and, more importantly, on student writing.

To improve scores on the open-response questions, we linked the comprehension strategies that teachers were already using during shared reading activities with MCAS practice. This was also the first year of our participation in the Read Excellence grant, which was awarded to our school by the Massachusetts Department of Education for three years and enabled us to work with reading experts from Tufts University. As part of this initiative, students worked in guided reading groups and wrote in open-response journals. Our hypothesis was that this would give students practice in going back into a story to find details to support their answers. In order to gain more than two of the four points available on each open-response question, students had to use details from the selection. Once again, our efforts were validated. The results of the 2002 MCAS indicated improvement on the open-response section of the English/Language Arts test (see Fig. 2). Fewer students were leaving their answers blank and more were scoring two or more points, indicating that they were going back into the stories to support their answers with evidence.

In response to our findings about oral reading, we are currently looking at research in the area of reading comprehension. Our working hypothesis is that fluency and oral language will be key to improving comprehension for our 3rd- and 4th-

FIGURE 2   Distribution of English/Language Arts open-response scores, 2001 and 2002

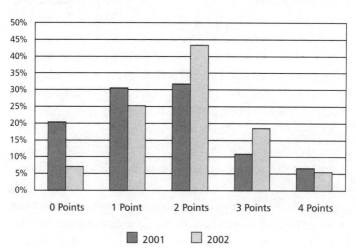

graders. Additional vocabulary development and oral language activities thus will be a priority in teaching our English-language learners.

Finally, our school improvement plan for the 2003-04 school year is based in large part on the data we have extracted from MCAS results. One area of student performance we will target during the coming year is open-response questions in math. Having seen an improvement in ELA open-response results with the use of journals, we hope to use math journals to accomplish similar success next year.

IMPLICATIONS FOR EDUCATORS

Our initial purpose in conducting this research was to document evidence of student learning despite disappointing test results. A logical extension of this effort was to look at where our students needed the most help and to see if we could improve instruction in those areas. Putting the information into graphs and explaining the data to faculty and staff redirected the conversations about instruction that were taking place in school. In the second year of our project we began to share the data with parents and incorporated it into our Unified School Improvement Plan. Educators who have access to detailed standardized test data can replicate virtually all of these efforts.

Doing action research allows educators to refine and shape a school's curriculum. In a test-driven climate that can be extremely stressful and sometimes even demoralizing, action research gives teachers an opportunity to focus their energy in positive ways and to improve their own practices. It encourages us as professionals to question our assumptions, to listen to our students, and to monitor testing data in ways that will help us better educate the young people who sit before us.

This chapter originally appeared in the Harvard Education Letter's *"Teacher Research" column in July/August 2003.*

The Larger Questions:
Weighing the Costs
and Benefits

Are High-Stakes Tests Worth the Wager?

Amid reports of test-score gains, researchers ask some tough questions

By Michael Sadowski

Choose the best answer to complete the following sentence: Standardized tests that are linked to graduation, promotion, and other high-stakes outcomes are . . .

a) a good idea because they create incentives for students, teachers, and schools to meet high achievement standards.

b) a good idea because they help to ensure that all students will graduate with at least a basic foundation of academic skills.

c) a bad idea because they stigmatize students who do poorly and exacerbate educational inequities along socioeconomic, racial, and ethnic lines.

d) a bad idea because they encourage a curriculum driven by fact memorization and test-taking "tricks" instead of critical thinking and other higher-order skills.

Poll the staff of any elementary, middle, or high school and you will probably get the full range of responses to this question in equal numbers. Similarly, education researchers are far from reaching a consensus about whether testing students for high-stakes outcomes actually improves learning. While some researchers seem to focus primarily on the potential and others on the pitfalls, many seem to agree that some key questions are not being asked in the current rush toward high-stakes testing. According to the latest figures released by the Education Commission of the States, a bipartisan policy group, more than half of U.S. states now require students to pass exit tests before they receive their high school diplomas.

In addition, the Bush administration's No Child Left Behind (NCLB) legislation, signed into law in 2002, has ushered in another wave of testing that has dramatically raised the stakes for every public school in every district across the U.S. Those schools that fail to demonstrate "adequate yearly progress" by posting higher scores for every identified student subgroup will be subject to sanctions that can range from required professional development to state takeover.

Testing appears to be popular with the vast majority of Americans: In a 2001 Gallup Poll, 77 percent of those surveyed said they approve of requiring students to pass tests for promotion from grade to grade. Why are testing programs so attractive to the general public? In part because they have a largely unquestioned reputation for objectivity, says Aaron M. Pallas, professor of sociology and education at Teachers College, Columbia University, and co-author of a report on high-stakes testing for the Civil Rights Project at Harvard University. "Most standardized tests are viewed by the public at large as objective, which means several things: there are right and wrong answers to the test questions, unlike grades, which are awarded at the 'whim' of a teacher; standardized tests are standardized—scores don't depend on who is performing the assessment; tests yield numerical scores, which are precise measures of performance; and, like a laboratory measurement, test scores are reliable. Testing experts acknowledge that some of these assumptions are questionable," says Pallas. "Test construction is a social and political process, and we cannot afford to lose sight of that fact."

Indeed, policymakers have responded to—if not partly created—the public appetite for high-stakes testing as more and more states and cities implement high school graduation tests, grade promotion exams, and the accountability programs required under NCLB. Two testing programs that have been studied widely in recent years—and have sparked considerable controversy—are those in Texas and Chicago.

TEXAS MIRACLE OR MIRAGE?

Among both proponents and detractors of high-stakes testing, Texas' history with statewide assessments over the past 13 years is frequently cited as a case in point. Education was the single most important issue to voters in the 2000 election, according to a Gallup Poll that year, and when former Texas Governor George W. Bush entered the White House in January 2001, the Lone Star State's assessment program attracted widespread attention.

The Texas Assessment of Academic Skills (TAAS), a group of tests taken in grades 3–8 and required for graduation, resulted in steadily rising scores over the 12 years it was administered from 1990-2002. Supporters of such testing programs heralded this success as the "Texas miracle," pointing out that not only did overall scores rise, but the performance of African American and Hispanic students also improved dramatically. While scores for White students rose 23 percent from 1994-2002, those for Hispanic students and students classified as "economically disadvantaged" rose 39 percent, and African American students' scores went up 44 percent over the same period.

Texas educators also received good news in a report issued in 2000 by the RAND research organization. RAND's study ranked the state second (only to North Carolina) among 44 states for its score gains on the National Assessment of Educational Progress (NAEP), a test that is often used as a benchmark against which claims of state-level achievement gains can be evaluated. That year, Laura Bush cited the RAND report at the Republican National Convention in Philadelphia and noted that "education reforms in Texas have resulted in some of the highest achievement gains in the country among all racial, socioeconomic, and family backgrounds."

In 2003, partly in preparation for the new accountability requirements of NCLB, the TAAS was replaced by the similarly named TAKS, the Texas Assessment of Knowledge and Skills, which state education officials claim is a more difficult test. "That's pretty much the hallmark of a successful system, that you outgrow your test . . . and you have to evolve to a more rigorous system and a system with more breadth," said Criss Cloudt, the Texas Education Agency's associate commissioner for policy planning and research, in the *Houston Chronicle.* Some observers, such as the conservative Texas Public Policy Foundation, have disputed the claim that the TAKS is significantly different from or more difficult than the TAAS. TAKS scores for 2003 were still being calculated at press time, but Cloudt noted that lower average scores are to be expected whenever a state implements a new testing program.

Critics, however, have long said that if a state starts with low scores on an assessment and then raises them over time, this does not prove that student learning is actually improving; it may just mean that students are getting better at taking that particular test. "Texas has made much of its claims of narrowing test-score gaps, but there is a lack of evidence of improvement except for the tests taught to," says Monty Neill, executive director of the National Center for Fair and Open Testing (FairTest) in Cambridge, Mass. As for the 2000 RAND report on Texas NAEP scores, Neill says it painted an incomplete picture because, as RAND has acknowledged, it did not include data from all testing years and was heavily weighted toward mathematics. "One has to be careful of these kinds of analyses when they leave out reading," Neill says. "The data certainly suggest that the vaunted gains the TAAS is supposed to [have created] do not show up elsewhere, except possibly in math."

Other researchers have noted that SAT scores for Texas students do not show the same gains in achievement that are evident on the TAAS. Whatever students' scores on the NAEP, TAAS, TAKS, or SAT, however, Neill is quick to add that these kinds of tests are hardly adequate measures of what students should know and be able to do: "Though it is very hard to track, we should be asking ourselves instead what our schools do that makes a difference in terms of real-world outcomes."

Researchers have also suggested that the passing rates on Texas' standardized tests tell only half the story. The other half, they say, can be found in the state's dropout and grade retention statistics for the years during which the TAAS was administered. For example, in a 2000 report for the National Board on Educational Testing and Public Policy at Boston College, authors Marguerite Clarke, Walter Haney, and George Madaus noted that high school dropout rates in Texas, particularly among minority students, rose considerably when the TAAS was implemented. The researchers also speculated that there may have been some connection between the attrition figures and the high-stakes assessments. They cited previous research by Haney that showed minor fluctuations in high school completion rates through the late 1970s and 1980s, but a sudden, sharp decline in the 1990–1991 school year, the first year the TAAS was required for graduation.

According to Haney's findings, based on Texas Education Agency statistics, about 60 percent of all black and Hispanic 9th graders in Texas went on to complete high school on schedule through most of the late 1970s and early 1980s, but in the years under TAAS, the numbers for each group hovered around 50 percent or slightly lower. White students graduated on schedule at a rate of about 70 percent in 1998 (the last year for which data were available at the time of the report), down slightly from the 72–78 percent range of figures seen in the late 1970s and early 1980s.

Also significant, the researchers said, were the state's retention statistics for 9th grade, the year before students were required to take the exit-level TAAS. According to Texas Education Agency data, the 9th-grade retention rate was dramatically higher than the rate for all other grade levels through most of the 1990s. For example, 18 percent of all 9th graders in Texas were retained at that level in 1997, and roughly one in four African American and Latino students were held back at this level. By contrast, only 2 percent of 8th graders, 8 percent of 10th graders, 5 percent of 11th graders, and 4 percent of 12th graders were retained. While it is difficult to draw conclusions about the reasons for the high 9th-grade retention rate, some have suggested that the TAAS was a major contributing factor.

At a 2000 Harvard Graduate School of Education forum on high-stakes testing, Angela Valenzuela, an associate professor at the University of Texas at Austin, suggested that weaker students were being held at the 9th-grade level so that they would not lower their schools' average scores. "The state's accountability system was originally designed to hold school administrators and teachers accountable, but the main people who are being punished here are the children," Valenzuela said.

DISPLACEMENT AND DISTORTION

Some researchers have also documented what they consider to be the detrimental effects of the Texas tests on curriculum. Linda M. McNeil, professor of education and director of the Center for Education at Rice University, has studied the effects of testing on Texas schools and sees in her case studies a pattern of "displacement and distortion" of curriculum to make way for test preparation. "There are classrooms where children read no prose from September to February," she says. Instead, McNeil adds, students read short, disconnected passages and answer questions about them in patterns similar to those seen on the exams. "They study information they are meant to forget. It's all artificial content to raise test scores."

Curriculum changes, McNeil says, when superintendents and school boards respond to political pressure to raise test scores by passing that pressure on to teachers and building-level administrators. A study by James V. Hoffman, Lori Assaf, and Julie Pennington of the University of Texas at Austin and Scott G. Paris of the University of Michigan supports this finding. In their survey of 200 Texas teachers, 85 percent agreed that areas not directly tested on the state assessments "receive less and less attention in the curriculum." The modification of curriculum is affecting poor and minority youth the most, says McNeil, since many of them attend schools where scores are lowest and the pressure to raise them is greatest. "[Students of color] are not getting the same educational experience as kids in suburban schools," she says.

Finally, the tests pose special challenges to the large number of Latino students in Texas for whom English is their second language. Catherine E. Snow, a professor at the Harvard Graduate School of Education and an expert in language and literacy development, says standardized tests present a conundrum regarding the inclusion of these second-language students: "We can't ask questions about how these tests affect language-minority kids unless we include them, but how do we do this without bringing negative consequences down on them?"

Despite such complications, however, some researchers contend that a test-driven curriculum is better than no real curriculum at all. Lauren Resnick, a faculty member at the University of Pittsburgh, has done extensive work in the areas of standards and accountability. While agreeing that "teaching to the test" is not the most effective approach to instruction, Resnick suggests that testing offers a kind of structure and coherence that is lacking in some teachers' classrooms, especially those teaching in poorly funded schools. "There are certainly some places where the curriculum is being dramatically narrowed to whatever types of items are on the test," Resnick says. "There are also places that five years ago were hardly teaching kids at all, especially poor kids. So now at least they're teaching them something, and it appears this is coming in the wake of high-stakes testing."

CHICAGO HOPE?

Another closely watched testing program was implemented in the Chicago Public Schools beginning with the 1996–1997 school year. Under the policy, Chicago 3rd-, 6th-, and 8th-grade students were required to achieve a certain cut score on the Iowa Test of Basic Skills (ITBS) in reading and mathematics in order to advance to the next grade. Because of low baseline test scores among Chicago students, school officials originally set the score requirements for promotion at one year below grade level for grade three, 1.5 years below grade level for grade six, and 1.8 years below grade level for grade eight. Students who did not meet the required score had to attend a six-week program called Summer Bridge and repeat the test at the end of the summer. If they failed the test again, they were retained in grade for that year. (School officials made exceptions to the policy for students participating in bilingual and special education programs.)

In a study called "Ending Social Promotion: Results from the First Two Years," researchers from the Consortium on Chicago School Research reported encouraging preliminary results. The data showed that ITBS scores improved significantly, with 20 percent more 6th graders and 21 percent more 8th graders reaching the minimum cut score in 1997 than in 1995 (before the scores were used as promotion criteria). The evidence suggested that the high stakes of the tests and the remediation programs were in some way combining to help students raise their scores, the researchers said. In addition, an update of the Consortium's report published in 2000 showed a continued, steady rise in ITBS scores.

Still, education researchers have been reluctant to call for an end to social promotion based on the Chicago experience. Jay P. Heubert, associate professor of education and law at Columbia University, notes that the news we get from research about grade retention is almost all bad: "Nearly all of the research on retention shows that it has strong negative effects on kids," he says. Heubert and Robert M. Hauser, a sociology professor at the University of Wisconsin-Madison, cite numerous studies on the effects of retention in a National Research Council report they edited, entitled *High Stakes: Testing for Tracking, Promotion, and Graduation*. The preponderance of studies, they note, link retention to such negative student outcomes as lower levels of academic and social success and much higher risk of dropping out.

Also, the Chicago Consortium's findings, though impressive in terms of test scores, have suggested that retention may be having a detrimental effect on some Chicago students. In their first report, the Consortium noted that "only one-fourth of retained 8th graders and one-third of retained 3rd and 6th graders in 1997 made 'normal' progress during the following school year, meaning that they stayed in the school system, were again subject to the policy, and passed the test cutoff the next May." For the group's updated report in 2000, researchers tracked retained students' progress over three years and compared it with that of students who had been socially promoted before the policy took effect. The Consortium found that "retained students [were] showing smaller achievement gains than previously socially promoted students."

Like the increase in TAAS scores, the Chicago students' rising scores on the ITBS have also led researchers to wonder if they represent real gains in academic skill or just improved test-taking ability. The data are inconclusive, but lend some support to the latter hypothesis. According to the Consortium, "The picture is mixed on whether getting students up to a test-score cutoff in one year allows them to do better the next year."

The Chicago testing program has also been criticized for perceived racial and ethnic discrimination. In 1999, Parents United for Responsible Education (PURE), a Chicago advocacy group, filed a complaint with the U.S. Department of Education's Office for Civil Rights (OCR), charging that the school system's use of the ITBS as a sole promotion criterion had a disproportionately negative effect on African American, Latino, and male students. After an OCR investigation, PURE won its claim. Since 1999, Chicago has continued to use the ITBS and to require underperforming students to attend summer school, but the test is now one of several criteria used to determine whether a student is promoted or retained.

Finally, Heubert notes that the company that publishes the ITBS, Riverside Publishing, has said that the tests are invalid for retention and promotion decisions. Heubert says, "Chicago is failing tens of thousands of kids each year, almost all minority and almost all likely dropouts, and the top brass knows the test they're using isn't even valid." Philip Hansen, chief accountability officer for the Chicago Public Schools, disputes that claim: "There's no evidence our promotion policy doesn't work, but those who are philosophically opposed to standardized tests will blast anything we do."

EXPERT GUIDELINES

Even those researchers who are holding high-stakes testing programs up to the closest scrutiny insist they are not against testing; they simply want a more critical review of its results and a more careful consideration of all its consequences. "Used properly, tests can be very helpful. Used poorly, they can do considerable harm," says Heubert.

To provide guidance to educators and policymakers on the fair and appropriate use of testing, the American Educational Research Association issued a position statement in 2000 outlining a set of conditions that should be met by any educational testing program (see Appendix B). These include using more than a single test for making high-stakes decisions about students, the provision of adequate resources and opportunities to learn, the alignment of tests with curriculum, and the full disclosure of the likely negative consequences of testing. The U.S. Department of Education's Office for Civil Rights also has published a resource guide on the use of high-stakes testing for educators and policymakers. It focuses on considerations for appropriate test use and the legal ramifications of high-stakes testing, especially those affecting second-language learners and students with disabilities.

"Tests can be a valuable part of a student's education," says Marguerite Clarke, associate director of the National Board on Educational Testing and Public Policy. "But when they become the driving force behind educational reform they can become corrupted. In this kind of environment, attention focuses almost exclusively on the test at the expense of other aspects of the education system. High-stakes testing can then lead to low-level learning." That's an outcome a public hungry for accountability may not be able to stomach.

This chapter, which has been edited for this volume, originally appeared in the September/October 2000 issue of the Harvard Education Letter. *It received an honorable mention (2nd place) for best newlsetter article in the 2001 National Press Club awards competition.*

FOR FURTHER INFORMATION

M. Clarke, W. Haney, and G. Madaus. "High Stakes Testing and High School Completion." Chestnut Hill, Mass.: Boston College, National Board on Educational Testing and Public Policy, January 2000. Available online at www.bc.edu/research/nbetpp/reports.html

R.F. Elmore and R. Rothman, eds. *Testing, Teaching, and Learning: A Guide for States and School Districts.* Washington, D.C.: National Research Council, 1999.

J.P. Heubert and R.M. Hauser, eds. *High Stakes: Testing for Tracking, Promotion, and Graduation.* Washington, D.C.: National Research Council, 1999.

J.V. Hoffman, L. Assaf, J. Pennington, and S.G. Paris. "High-Stakes Testing in Reading: Today in Texas, Tomorrow?" *The Reading Teacher* 54, no. 5: 482–492.

M. Markley. "Time's Up for the TAAS." *Houston Chronicle*, March 9, 2003. Available online at www.chron.com/cs/CDA/printstory.hts/special/schools/03/1804557

L.M. McNeil. "Creating New Inequalities: Contradictions of Reform." *Phi Delta Kappan* 81, no. 10 (June 2000): 729–734.

M. Roderick, A.S. Bryk, B.A. Jacob, J.Q. Easton, and E. Allensworth. "Ending Social Promotion: Results from the First Two Years." Chicago: Consortium on Chicago School Research, December 1999. Available online at www.consortium-chicago.org/publications/p0g04.html

M. Roderick, M. Engel, and J. Nagaoka. "Ending Social Promotion: Results from Summer Bridge." Chicago: Consortium on Chicago School Research, February 2003. Available online at www.consortium-chicago.org/publications/p59.html

M. Roderick, J. Nagaoka, J. Bacon, and J.Q. Easton. "Update: Ending Social Promotion—Passing, Retention, and Achievement Trends among Promoted and Retained Students, 1995–1999." Chicago: Consortium on Chicago School Research, September 2000. Available online at www.consortium-chicago.org/publications/p0g01.html

U.S. Department of Education, Office for Civil Rights. "The Use of Tests as Part of High-Stakes Decision-Making for Students: A Resource Guide for Educators and Policy-makers." Available online at www.ed.gov/offices/OCR/testing

Why Current Assessments Don't Measure Up

Tests need to accommodate diverse learners and approaches

By Marya R. Levenson

Statewide standards that emphasize accountability for all students have challenged educators to look more closely at student data to see who is learning and who is struggling to learn. Considering the skills our students will need to compete in tomorrow's economy, many of us can appreciate the need for more demanding graduation requirements for all students. For too many years, educators and parents have not had high enough expectations for poor urban and rural students, and even for some students in affluent suburbs.

What administrators and teachers are discovering, however, is that mandating standards does not, by itself, raise achievement. Some educators and parents are questioning whether current assessments such as standardized tests are adequate for showing how students and schools measure up to the new standards. Furthermore, the new federal legislation, No Child Left Behind (NCLB), now threatens the fragile consensus that had begun to build around state standards and assessments.

CHALLENGES IN TEACHING DIVERSE STUDENTS

The fact that NCLB requires schools to report on how sub-groups of students perform means that many schools are now increasingly focused on how to raise the test scores of students who receive free or reduced-price lunches, have disabilities, or are identified as English language learners. But students come into schools with very different backgrounds and preparations. Some of these children face incredible hardship as they and their families grapple with poverty, illness, or other problems. Others do not learn well in traditional classrooms. In order to have a chance to achieve at a higher level, they may need alternative teaching and learning approaches, more individual attention, or more time to master a subject.

As suburban and rural schools have developed a variety of instructional programs to teach students who don't do well in traditional classrooms, we have learned that many students are capable of achieving much more than we had previously believed possible. One such program in a suburban Upstate New York district, the Integrated Regents Program at Shaker High School outside Albany, provides interdisciplinary instruction for students who learn better through problem-solving. City districts also are reporting academic gains through the use of reading and math coaches, who are helping teachers use articulated elementary and middle school curricula. Elsewhere, large high schools are being divided into small schools to personalize learning.

Such programs, however, require extra time and resources, two things that are in short supply under most of the new accountability and assessment systems. Teachers working in smaller classes need time to develop and modify new curricula and instruction to facilitate good learning *and* acceptable re-sults on new state exams. There is also much concern among educators that some students will not be able to reach new learning standards on the tight timetables set by many states— even where transitional safety nets such as lower passing scores are temporarily in place. And in large urban districts where too many uncertified teachers work in challenging situations with-out sufficient staff development and curricula, the students being denied high school diplomas are paying a high price for system failures. (In Massachusetts, it is outrageous that some policymakers are proud that *only* 10,000 students failed to graduate in June 2003.)

Some who are advocating for higher standards have not been so quick to advocate for the additional resources needed, espe-cially in urban and poor rural districts, to support staff and pro-gram development. Even states like Massachusetts that have increased district fiscal resources as part of their education re-form initiatives have been hard pressed to maintain this sup-port during the continuing fiscal downturn.

In this context, NCLB is a ticking time bomb that may in fact penalize states that have developed higher standards. Be-cause states that have higher academic standards and more difficult assessments will probably have a higher percentage of failing students and schools, some states are considering lower-ing their passing cutoff scores. And neither the federal nor state governments have begun to grapple with the fiscal and other implications of the new NCLB mandate for yearly testing of students in grades 3–8. Nor have they addressed the fact that current standardized assessments are not adequate for measur-ing students' knowledge of complex new learning standards.

MULTIPLE, DIVERSE MEASURES ARE NEEDED

State departments of education understandably want to have "foolproof" assessments to indicate how schools are meeting new standards, ones that can withstand challenges by angry parents or state legislators when many children fail to pass. (Even though several states and testing companies have recently had to admit to some errors in scoring and setting cutoff scores, they continue to insist on the validity and reliability of their standardized tests.) States and the federal government also place a premium on standardization so that schools can be compared to one another. As a result, the application of rich and complex learning standards is being undermined by the use of high-stakes standardized tests.

For example, many New York State teachers have become so focused on preparing 4th- and 8th-grade students for publisher-developed English-language arts and mathematics tests that they no longer develop creative, in-depth performance assessments in these and other subjects. Moreover, because of the incredible pressure caused by these tests and the numerous articles and editorials comparing school and district results, many 4th and 5th graders believe that they are failures because of poor initial test results. Some 4th and 8th graders are even being retained based on test scores, despite the fact that these new assessments were originally implemented to alert schools and families to which students needed more support in order to pass Regents exams years later in high school.

These pressures will undoubtedly increase with the new yearly testing mandated by the federal government, where the judgment about whether a school fails (and thus loses fiscal resources) will depend not on its mean or median test results, but on the "average yearly progress" of all subgroups. Another sad, unanticipated consequence of NCLB may be that not only students and parents but experienced good teachers may leave urban schools where they are most needed, rather than remain in schools that will lose resources and be labeled in the press as "failing."

Standardized tests can provide a good snapshot of how our students and districts perform compared to others in the state and the nation. But as the American Educational Research Association has declared, it is inappropriate and ill advised to judge a student's performance based on one standardized test (see Appendix B). Instead, multiple measures, including classwork and teacher evaluations, should be part of any informed judgment about a student's skill level. At this time, when NCLB is encouraging the use of state standardized tests as the only criterion for judging schools (and therefore students), educators and politicians need to advocate for multiple measures to assess whether a student has truly met learning standards.

One additional cautionary note: As schools focus on helping students who were previously allowed to "get by" reach higher levels of achievement, we also need to maintain appropriate standards and assessments for high-achieving students. It would be truly ironic if efforts to implement "higher" state standards ended up diluting or weakening the educational experiences of the many students who already meet or exceed those standards.

Creating and implementing high educational standards is an essential challenge. Never before in our country's history have we attempted to have all high school students attain such high levels of literacy and other skills. Implementing new standards incorrectly or too quickly can harm our children and our schools. As schools work to meet these ambitious standards, incremental accomplishments should be recognized; we should not be penalizing schools because all student subgroups did not make a certain percentage of progress on standardized tests each year. Since teachers understandably focus what they teach on how their students will be assessed, let's make the assessments worthy measures of the new learning standards.

This commentary originally appeared in the Harvard Education Letter's *March/April 2000 issue. It has been edited for this volume.*

My Lunch with Jackie

How a much-maligned test is holding schools and families accountable

By Jeff Howard

had a luncheon meeting a few weeks ago with an old friend, a thoughtful, successful African American woman. We were discussing education issues, but when the conversation turned to the MCAS (the Massachusetts Comprehensive Assessment System, our state proficiency test) it hit a snag. "I must admit," she declared, "I'm ambivalent about the MCAS." She articulated two reasons. First, she feared the test was forcing teachers to "teach to the test," thus stultifying instruction and restricting the range of curricula being used in the schools. Second, she was afraid it was putting an unfair burden of accountability on kids for the failures of the schools (the class of 2003 was the first required to pass the MCAS as a condition for graduating), without any such burden on the adults who were, in fact, responsible for the failure.

Now, I regard the MCAS (and tests like it in most of the other states) as the best, most hopeful thing to happen in public education in the twenty years I have been actively engaged in it. The tests have shaken up a public education regime that until lately had proven just about impervious to intervention. Otherwise responsible adults in schools, community institutions, and universities have for years—sometimes for entire careers—

conceded to the apparently unfathomable complexity of educational change. Good people in each of these sectors have been unwilling, sometimes defiantly unwilling, to accept responsibility. I have heard educators make outrageous statements, such as, "I taught the material, they just didn't learn it," without shame, in large meetings before hundreds of other teachers. For many years I have been dismayed by the extreme apathy of parents and community leaders, in cities across the country, ineffectual in the face of schools annually turning out tens of thousands of kids barely able to read, and therefore with little realistic prospect of being able to learn later what the legitimate economy requires. Everyone—educators, parents, and community leaders—has seemed content to shirk his or her own responsibility under cover of fingers pointed at other parties. But pointed fingers provide poor shelter. The "somebody should do something" act had gotten very old after a couple of years, but it went on numbingly for decades, while majorities of successive generations of kids in our cities (and many in suburbs and rural areas, too) were left with the choice of dropping out or hanging in long enough to graduate with inadequate skills and worthless diplomas. Then, a couple of years ago, it all started to change.

Absent effective initiatives coming from inside public education, a group of outsiders—business leaders, governors, and pragmatic school reformers from around the country—took the situation in hand. They developed templates for criterion-referenced proficiency tests (CRTs) that were introduced, first in a few states, then in rapid succession in almost all of the others. CRTs represent an approach to assessment radically different from the old norm-referenced tests (NRTs), which compared children to one another and were designed to distinguish winners from losers. By definition, fully half of NRT takers are destined to be regarded as losers, since it is preordained that half will perform below the norm. CRTs, on the other hand, are organized around a standard, *proficiency*, not a norm. Proficiency is defined as demonstrated knowledge and application skills in a given subject. A proficient child knows the material and can use it in new and novel situations. Tests of proficiency are based on a liberating assumption—that all children can, theoretically, rise to the proficiency standard: "Listen up, boys and girls. This is a game everyone can win. *There need not be losers here.*" A CRT represents a target, and with a little confidence building, an enticing one. It holds out the promise that with access to good, aligned curricula, flexible instructional approaches, and lots of hard work, children can achieve proficiency.

And the new tests do something else: they set a clear standard for the adults in charge, a measuring stick for how well *we* are doing. What percentage of our kids hit the proficiency standard? What is the rate of improvement from one test administration to the next? Are there proficiency gaps between children from different population groups? And in all these measures, how does our performance, our rate of improvement, compare with other classrooms, schools, and communities? These are interesting questions indeed, made possible by standardized assessment tools administered to all children at a given grade level, at the same time. And make no mistake: the answers shine a light of accountability squarely on adults. They are powerful measures of *adult proficiency*, defined as the demonstrated capacity, without excuses, to move children to proficiency in all their subjects, at all grade levels. There is an implicit assumption operating in the standards movement that children's academic performance directly reflects the quality of adult management of education.

As you might imagine, not everyone is thrilled by the prospect of being measured in this way. Some teacher unions have resisted to the point of mounting expensive television ad campaigns, focusing on the damage testing does to children. Some school reformers (often headquartered in the universities) deplore the deadening effects on good teaching they believe will result from the tests, and the distraction from their own preferred approach to education reform, teacher retraining and certification. Some parent and community leaders, suspicious of the motivations of the testers, work to protect their children from one more potential failure at the hands of "the man." And the woods are full of professional test-bashers, who seem to have an ideological aversion to the idea of any assessment of human beings (one wonders how they've responded to state requirements for obtaining a driver's license—talk about high stakes testing!). The objections of these various opponents have filled the air with indistinct forebodings about the tests. Good people who lack the means to really investigate these rather technical issues and evaluate competing claims find themselves "ambivalent."

My friend listened to my (somewhat practiced) responses to her objections to the MCAS: 1) The "teaching to the test" complaint is overstated. The graduation requirement (one point above failing on a 10th grade test) is so low that it is extremely unlikely that creative, effective teachers all over the state are really being forced to forego Shakespeare, unless they are doing so to make a point. What is far more likely is that poorly trained and poorly supervised teachers, who have never been given an adequate sense of what they were supposed to be doing, are, for the first time, getting a clear standard to shoot for, and guidelines they can use to structure their teaching. 2) While Massachusetts has made student accountability, in the form of the

MCAS graduation requirement, first on the agenda (I believe a difficult, but justifiable, decision by policymakers), it has also established a mechanism for adult accountability, the Educational Management Audit Council,[1] to evaluate the performance of school systems around the state, using disaggregated student MCAS scores to measure adult performance. In the coming months and years, we will see serious consequences for school systems and communities that continue to show poor student performance.

Jackie was attentive to my argument, but I could tell she was not exactly inspired by it, so we moved on. Several topics later, toward the end of our lunch, she remembered something she had wanted to tell me. It turns out there is an education initiative being launched by black parents in her own (affluent) suburban community focused on black student performance. An analysis of the MCAS scores of different population groups in their schools turned up some interesting facts: although the overall performance of the community's children was very high, black children as a group scored significantly lower than whites, in both reading and math, at every grade level. The black parents had become very alarmed (and perhaps a little angry) about this, and were now organized and in active discussion with school officials about "closing the gap."

At this point I fell back on my old training in clinical psychology and made an interpretation: My answers to Jackie's questions about the MCAS were technically correct but uninspiring, so on a less-than-conscious level she went to work to come up with a more compelling answer, in the form of her own story. It can be summed up simply: Data from well-constructed assessments of student learning can be a powerful

[1] I am one of five Governor-appointed members of this council.

agent of change. It has the capacity to focus and mobilize parents so that they can accurately monitor the performance of their children—and the adults who teach them. The standards give parents something to strive for (proficiency for their children), and the tests provide a way to assess the performance of adults in their children's schools and classrooms, as well as in their own families.

Tests like the MCAS are, at base, systems of accountability for states, communities, schools, and families. When good people can begin to exercise real responsibility for what is happening to their children in the schools, real change will follow. That may be the best argument of all for standards and assessments.

The Tests and
the Curriculum

Collateral Damage

**Social-justice curricula are jeopardized in
high-stakes environments**

By Lisa Birk

N athaniel, a factory worker, keeps warm by burning
worthless German marks. Teenage Sophie wishes Kai-
ser Wilhelm II would "come save us all." And Mary's
father has just joined the Nazi party. She is glad, she
writes, because she has been told "[the Nazis] have some good
ideas."

In Doc Miller's 8th-grade social studies class, it is Germany in the 1920s. The Treaty of Versailles is still fresh, and Ad-
olf Hitler's *Mein Kampf* is newly published. These Concord,
Mass., students are reading letters written in the voices of characters they have invented. They are integrating personal, social, and historical facts in an effort to understand the complex
dynamics that propelled Hitler to power. Miller, a 33-year veteran, is teaching from Facing History and Ourselves (FHAO),
a social-justice curriculum created in 1976 that is taught in
6,000 schools across the country. FHAO uses Holocaust studies to teach students the importance of critical thinking in understanding and protecting the rights and responsibilities of all.
As one of Miller's former students told his class, "This is so
important. You listen to this course."

And yet, says Miller, the increasing emphasis on preparing for state-mandated standardized tests such as the Massachusetts Comprehensive Assessment System (MCAS) makes it more challenging to use such curricula. "If you were going to go according to MCAS, I wouldn't have done anything you saw today," he says. The MCAS doesn't cover Germany from the 1920s to the 1940s. Many teachers with less seniority than Miller who were working in a less supportive system might be afraid to spend 10 weeks on content that would not show up on the state-mandated test. Even without standardized testing, many teachers might avoid teaching complex material, including social-justice curricula, because it is labor intensive. Standardized testing only makes it more difficult.

Wherever testing is state mandated, FHAO and social-justice curricula like it are jeopardized. In California, Tennessee, Illinois, Ohio, New York, and Massachusetts, some teachers are using FHAO on a modified basis, compressing the 10-week course into two weeks or transplanting elements to a different grade or subject, reports FHAO associate program director Alan Stoskopf. Sometimes, a shift to another grade level or subject area may be beneficial, but truncating the course can be disastrous. Some teachers have had to drop it altogether.

AT THE MARGINS

Paradoxically, state-mandated tests aim to enhance learning, teaching, and accountability, but in many cases may be hampering all three. Multiple-choice tests do not typically reward inquiry or analysis, so curricula that emphasize such in-depth learning are often relegated to the margins of the school day. Measuring the impact of such complex curricula as FHAO would require pre- and post-tests that measure student engagement, emotional maturity, thinking skills, and content. But leaders of such complex programs have trouble securing money, let alone developing reliable tests. Tom Roderick, executive director of the Metropolitan New York chapter of Educators for Social Responsibility (ESR), says that despite studies showing that ESR's conflict-resolution program reduces violence and improves test scores, resources for such "social/emotional training" have been cut significantly in recent years.

What constitutes a social-justice curriculum? The broadest definition spans a continuum from teaching interpersonal skills, such as good listening, to service learning to an analysis of social, political, and economic inequities. Whatever the approach to social-justice teaching, most theorists agree that its success depends not only on curricula but on whether teachers, schools, and school policies model and nurture fairness. In other words, "social-justice curriculum involves not only what we teach, but how we teach it," says Michael W. Apple, a professor of curriculum, instruction, and educational policy studies at the University of Wisconsin–Madison.

That kind of teaching requires time—time that preparing for standardized tests often doesn't allow. Says Doc Miller: "I am convinced, after 30 years of teaching, that you need to give time to thoughtfully go into things, to ask questions, to look at cause and effect, to understand [history] from a variety of viewpoints." Proponents of programs such as FHAO believe such time is well worth investing. They cite the needs of a democratic society for an informed and engaged citizenry. "Schooling . . . is not only about learning skills so you can get a job," says Roderick. "It's about thinking, asking questions, and understanding that citizens play a crucial role in deciding the most important issues of the day."

Such understanding may be needed now more than ever. In his book *Bowling Alone: The Collapse and Revival of American Community*, Harvard public policy researcher Robert D. Putnam documents a sharp decline in civic engagement and social trust since the early 1970s, while the country has become increasingly multicultural. If that is indeed true, then misunderstandings and conflict are perhaps inevitable without some help from public institutions of all kinds, including schools.

FEELING CONNECTED

One study suggests that social-justice curricula, with their emphasis on fairness, may promote healthy behaviors. Published in the *Journal of the American Medical Association* in 1997, the longitudinal study of 12,000 adolescents, grades 7 to 12, found two protective factors against risky behavior: feeling connected to family and feeling connected to school. "Parent-family connectedness and perceived school connectedness were protective against every health-risk behavior measure except history of pregnancy," wrote researcher Michael D. Resnick and his coauthors. When schools succeed in fostering such an atmosphere, students feel connected, and that connectedness is associated with lower levels of violent behavior and substance abuse, as well as a postponement of first-time sexual intercourse.

A two-year study of 5,000 students commissioned by ESR of its Resolving Conflict Creatively Program (RCCP) provides partial confirmation of those findings. Created in 1985, RCCP is a K–12 program based on the assumption that violence is learned and so can be unlearned. In that 1999 study, children who received substantial RCCP instruction tended to "see violence as an unacceptable option, and to choose competent strategies for resolving conflict rather than aggressive ones. They also did better academically," concluded principal investigator J. Lawrence Aber. ESR's Tom Roderick hypothesizes that academics improved because "working with the RCCP curriculum fosters better rapport between teachers and students, so the climate in the classroom is more positive and conducive to learning."

Social-justice learning and preparation for standardized testing don't have to be mutually exclusive. For example, six years ago, Hudson (Mass.) public schools superintendent Sheldon Berman tied service learning to district standards K–12. Six years later, Hudson's test scores are better, and its community ties are stronger. Service learning—a kind of applied social-justice program in which students combine volunteer experiences with analysis—offered rich opportunities for students in Hudson, an industrial town with a large bilingual population. For example, the district's 4th-grade science program includes a hands-on, inquiry-based wetlands curriculum. Students collect and classify samples, help clean up wetland areas and build nature trails, and learn the value of protecting fragile ecosystems. In 1998, those 4th graders scored in the top 20 percent on the state-mandated test. This year those scores dropped some, but they continue to have "strong and improving results on the California Achievement Test," according to Berman.

Of course, the real purpose of social-justice education is to help students get a better understanding of the world and their place in it. Facing History and Ourselves, which aims to link historical analysis and individual behavior, has been shown to decrease racism and fighting among students and to increase social maturity, according to two studies sponsored by the Carnegie Corporation of New York. In 1996, Carnegie funded a pair of two-year studies to evaluate the program, a large outcome study and a small qualitative case study. The first study compared the growth of 212 FHAO students with 134 comparison students. Teachers of the comparison students also emphasized intergroup relations, racism, and prejudice in their teaching, but they did not use FHAO.

The second analysis—an intensive case study of 19 FHAO students—found that half the students were able to draw connections between "the motivations and responses of individuals to the Nazis during the Holocaust" and the motivations of themselves or others today regarding social issues. One-third said in interviews that they had a better appreciation for how easily people can be seduced into wrongdoing. "Eighth graders are centrally concerned with figuring out where they fit and what belonging to a group means," says program evaluator Dennis Barr. "Issues of loyalty and conformity come up powerfully."

BLEAK FUTURE

Despite such promising results, the future of social-justice curricula looks bleak at a time when standardized testing—frequently described as a mile wide and an inch deep—has gained so much momentum. As Monty Neill, executive director of the National Center for Fair and Open Testing, points out, testing "is convenient. It reduces everything to a number." And that, he says, suits politicians and business leaders who are more concerned with creating a work force than fostering social justice.

Although 90 percent of teacher educators agree that core values should be taught in schools, only 13 percent are "satisfied" with their efforts, according to a 1999 study by the Boston

University Center for the Advancement of Ethics and Character. Why? Because, according to the report, the educators were "busy meeting their states' mandated content requirements."

This chapter originally appeared in the Harvard Education Letter's *March/April 2001 issue.*

FOR FURTHER INFORMATION

J.L. Aber, J.L. Brown, and C.C. Henrich. *Teaching Conflict Resolution: An Effective School-Based Approach to Violence Prevention.* New York: National Center for Children in Poverty, 1999. Available online at www.nccp.org/pub_tcr99.html

M.W. Apple and J.A. Beane. *Democratic Schools.* Alexandria, Va.: Association for Supervision and Curriculum Development, 1995.

S.H. Berman. "Service as Systemic Reform." *The School Administrator* 57, no. 7 (2000): 20–24.

Facing History and Ourselves, 16 Hurd Rd., Brookline, MA 02445; 617-232-1595; fax: 617-232-0281. www.facing.org

National Center for Fair and Open Testing, 342 Broadway, Cambridge, MA 02139; 617-864-4810; fax: 617-497-2224; email: info@fairtest.org.; website: www.fairtest.org

R.D. Putnam. *Bowling Alone: The Collapse and Revival of American Community.* New York: Simon & Schuster, 2000.

M.D. Resnick, P.S. Bearman et al. "Protecting Adolescents from Harm: Findings from the National Longitudinal Study on Adolescent Health." *Journal of the American Medical Association* 278, no. 10 (1997): 823–832.

K. Ryan and K. Bohlin. "Teacher Education's Empty Suit." *Education Week* (March 8, 2000): 41–42.

The Arts Step Out from the Wings

Can arts programs boost test scores? Should their survival depend on it?

By Jane Buchbinder

Editors' note: As we were selecting past HEL articles for inclusion in this volume, one of our colleagues suggested this piece from the November/December 1999 issue. When we reread the article, we were reminded of the excellent questions it raised about the role of the arts in raising student achievement. These considerations take on new meaning as schools prepare to meet all the demands of the No Child Left Behind legislation. Are schools eliminating arts programs to make way for more test preparation? If so, will such reprioritization necessarily result in higher scores? Jane Buchbinder's piece invites us to look beyond what may seem like the obvious answers to these and other questions.

Howard Gardner's theory of multiple intelligences has paved the way for a broader outlook on the contributions the arts make in the classroom. This cognitive psychologist has helped educators recognize that learning takes place through many means in addition to book reading, and that children are best served by having opportunities to gain and demonstrate their understanding in a variety of ways.

This relatively new way of viewing the arts—as a process embracing thoughts, emotions, and reason—has led some to hope that the arts can help repair the nation's education system. Proponents of arts education say the arts make learning more enjoyable and interactive, foster an interdisciplinary approach to learning, build self-esteem, teach critical thinking and self-discipline, and allow students with different learning styles and language skills to be successful in their own way.

With this in mind, research projects supported by corporate, foundation, and government offices are focused on three central questions: Are the arts aiding student achievement? Who has access to good arts programs? What do high-quality arts programs look like?

ACHIEVEMENT AND ACCESS

One well-regarded examination of the effects of the arts on achievement has been led by James Catterall of the University of California, Los Angeles. Looking at the results of the 1988 National Educational Longitudinal Survey (NELS), which tracked the progress of 25,000 middle and high school students over 10 years, Catterall found that students with "high arts involvement"—that is, those who took at least two arts classes per week and participated in extracurricular arts—performed far better on standardized tests than students with "low arts involvement." Of "high arts" 8th graders, 66.8 percent scored in the top half on standardized tests, compared with 42.7 percent of "low arts" students. By the 10th grade, 72.5 percent of those same "high arts" students scored in the top half on standardized tests, while just 45 percent of the "low arts" students did. That suggests that students involved in the arts have an advantage that grows with time and experience, according to Catterall.

Not surprisingly, the study also shows that students are twice as likely to have low arts involvement if they are of low socioeconomic status (SES)—that is, from less educated or less affluent households. Students from high-SES households typically enjoy many advantages—private art lessons, affluent school districts (where arts programs are more prevalent), access to transportation for afterschool arts activities, and the encouragement of parents who have themselves benefited from exposure to the arts.

Still, one noteworthy finding came from Catterall's comparison of low-SES students with either "high arts" or "low arts" involvement: the "high arts" students performed much better than their counterparts on standardized tests and in such subjects as math, reading, history, and geography.

If the arts are an important part of learning, say arts advocates and researchers, then they will need to be made available not just in affluent school districts or in a few less affluent schools chosen for research and experimentation, but across the board.

THE QUALITY QUESTION

Much arts education research is also focused on how to build quality arts programs. *Gaining the Arts Advantage*, a nationwide study issued by the President's Committee for the Arts and Humanities and the Arts Education Partnership (during the Clinton Administration), cites several common elements of the high-quality programs in the hundreds of school districts it surveyed. These include: community and parent involvement in school arts programs; opportunities and funding for student exhibitions and performances; written policies that affirm the value of the arts; top-rated artists in residence; and administrators and school boards that treat arts education the same as other subject areas, especially at budget-cutting time.

Districts that get hit hard at budget time can still succeed in building effective arts programs by using a little creativity, the report shows. Redondo Beach (Calif.) School District, for example, trains parents to assist in its elementary school arts programs, giving them a chance not only to learn more about the arts themselves, but also to build stronger ties to local schools. Another example is the Linwood A+ Elementary School in St. Paul, Minn., where founding principal Kris Peterson shrewdly hired a part-time grant writer who doubled as a vocal music instructor.

TEACHERS AS ARTISTS

Bringing teachers into the world of arts, and artists into the world of teaching, is another important element of successful programs. That's the focus of SUAVE (the Spanish acronym for United Community for Arts in Education), a research project directed by Merryl Goldberg of California State University, San Marcos. The program provides teachers with weekly in-class coaching from professional artists on ways to teach subjects such as math, science, language arts, and social studies through the arts. In addition, teachers get discounted tickets to arts events and professional development at arts centers. Goldberg's research, which consists of classroom observations and interviews with students and teachers, shows that the arts become another means of expression in the classroom—an important resource in a multilingual state like California.

"The teacher-artist relationship goes to the core not only of teacher learning, but [also] of teachers' relationships with their students, because teachers learn new ways of communicating content," says Goldberg. "Teachers in turn invest their students with the same skills. So kids who have trouble understanding or expressing themselves in English have an opportunity to fully participate in learning."

A wealth of anecdotal evidence from students, teachers, and administrators seems to confirm the notion that the arts can invigorate the learning process in a variety of ways. When Kathy Greeley's humanities class at the Graham and Parks School in Cambridge, Mass., creates a play, she challenges her students to incorporate local history and places in order to gain a better understanding of the world they live in. Nina Ward, 13, the lead actor in one of the plays Greeley directed about the construction of the American Dream, agrees: "When I have to show history through acting, I learn more because I kind of have to live it to explain it to myself."

Christopher Forehan, former principal of the multicultural Chavez Elementary School in Norwalk, Calif., which serves mostly low-income kids, says he didn't think much about what his students might gain from the arts. A pro-arts superintendent changed that, insisting that arts be given a bigger role in his district. With strong arts partnerships from the Getty Foundation and the Music Center of Los Angeles, the arts were blended into the Chavez School curriculum. The move changed Forehan's perception of the arts in education.

"As the principal, I had to be involved, and that's why I think it worked. We had total school involvement," he says, explaining that he participated in creative activities whenever there was a resident artist. "We learned to use descriptive words by focusing on a Monet painting. We used dance to describe the geography and plant life in our region. The kids worked with a writer and professional actors to create plays. That got them very excited and motivated. And that's how I learned to love the arts, too."

CAN THE ARTS BE MEASURED?

One of the most challenging questions facing arts advocates and researchers is how to evaluate arts programs. Last year, while calling into question several studies that claim to link arts education with achievement in other subjects, Elliot Eisner of Stanford argued in the pages of the journal *Art Education* against trying to make such links. "When such contributions become priorities," he wrote, "the arts become handmaidens to ends that are not distinctively artistic and in the process undermine the value of art's unique contributions to the education of the young."

Some scholars point to the Mozart Effect as a good example of what goes wrong when arts research is misunderstood. In 1993, researchers from the University of California, Irvine, suggested that college students who listen to Mozart have temporarily improved performances on spatial-temporal reasoning (especially valuable in math)—evidence that seemed to bolster the idea that the arts enhance learning in other disciplines. But an exaggerated interpretation by the press and policymakers of the findings turned it into one of the most misreported and misused studies in recent memory. The former governor of Georgia, for example, raised $100,000 in private funds to give families with newborns classical music CDs, in the hope of improving the future intellectual capacities of children.

Ellen Winner, professor of psychology at Boston College and senior research associate at Harvard's Project Zero, is countering what she calls "bogus reporting" with the Reviewing Education and the Arts Project (REAP), a reexamination of hundreds of arts studies from the 1950s to the present. Formerly an art student, Winner is an advocate for arts in education. Nonetheless, she says her study is finding more anecdotal evidence than hard scientific data about the link between arts and achievement.

Criticized within the pro-arts community for questioning the work of researchers, Winner says her motive is to set the arts on the sturdiest ground possible: their intrinsic merit. If arts programs live by the sword of rising test scores, they may die by that same sword, she contends. "If research ultimately refutes the arts' ability to raise academic test scores, people will say, 'Well, okay, we don't need the arts.'"

The difficulty of trying to scientifically document the value of the arts may itself be a measure of their educational depth and complexity, says Jessica Davis, founding director of the Arts in Education program at Harvard's Graduate School of Education. "If, in responding to a child's writing, you notice the emotional, expressive content and the intellectual excitement of the plot and say, 'This is very good, but I don't know how to measure it,' you're forced into the wrong conversation," she says.

By demanding conventional assessment measures for content that isn't easily tested, policymakers may be hindering the development of vital programs in the arts, as well as in math, English, history, and science, arts advocates say. Perhaps this is part of the reason that spending on the arts makes up a small percentage of elementary and secondary school budgets.

THE BIG DISCONNECT

In fact, despite all the good press that school arts programs have gotten, the arts still have only a marginal presence in mainstream education. Arts-friendly districts are the exception, not the rule, says Project Zero director Steve Seidel. "There are lots of voices talking about the importance of the arts in education, but there's a big disconnect in action," he says. "One reason is that models of high-quality arts-in-schools programs are not commonplace enough. Like any advance in education, it is difficult to design a program that is highly effective. Good arts programs require a sustained effort, sustained resources, an actively involved community, and significant professional development. And all that doesn't come together often enough."

As researchers continue to examine the role the arts can play in educating young people, practitioners who are already convinced—often by their own experiences—that the arts have an essential place in the classroom aren't waiting for "hard" evidence. Jackie Frisbee, principal at the Hanna Woods Elementary School in Chesterton, Mo., says she can see for herself how beneficial her school's arts programs are: "I see them teaching kids respect for talent and creativity, both their own and that of others. And that increases their love of learning. My feeling is that the arts enrich a student's whole life."

That goes to the heart of what schooling is all about, says Project Zero's Steve Seidel. "The job of education is to be engaging and challenging, to address important issues in human experience, to inspire children to think hard, and to provide them the opportunity to demonstrate what they've learned. Seems a shame not to link the two enterprises."

This chapter originally appeared in the Harvard Education Letter's *November/December 1999 issue. It has been edited for this volume.*

FOR FURTHER INFORMATION

ArtsEdge, The John F. Kennedy Center for the Performing Arts, Washington, DC 20566; 202-416-8871. artsedge.kennedy-center.org/artsedge.html

Arts Education Partnership, One Massachusetts Ave., NW, Washington, DC 20001-1431; 202-326-8693. www.aep-arts.org

J.S. Catterall. "Does Experience in the Arts Boost Academic Achievement? A Response to Eisner." *Art Education* 51, no. 4 (July 1998): 6-11.

E.W. Eisner. "Does Experience in the Arts Boost Academic Achievement?" *Art Education* 51, no. 1 (January 1998): 7-15.

E.B. Fiske. "Champions of Change: The Impact of the Arts on Learning." President's Committee on the Arts and Humanities, 1100 Pennsylvania Ave., NW, Suite 526, Washington, DC 20506; 202-682-5409. www.pcah.gov

M. Goldberg. *Arts and Learning: An Integrated Approach to Teaching and Learning in Multicultural and Multilingual Settings*. New York: Longman, 1997.

M.R. Goldberg and A. Phillips, eds. *Arts as Education* (Harvard Educational Review Reprint Series, No. 24). Cambridge, Mass.: Harvard Educational Review, 1992.

L. Longley. "Champions of Change: Lessons from School Districts That Value Arts Education." President's Committee on the Arts and Humanities, 1100 Pennsylvania Ave., NW, Suite 526, Washington, DC 20506; 202-682-5409. www.pcah.gov

National Arts Education Association, 1916 Association Dr., Reston, VA 20191-1590; 703-860-8000. www.naea-reston.org

Project Zero, Harvard Graduate School of Education, 124 Mount Auburn Street, 5th Floor, Cambridge, MA 02138. pzweb.harvard.edu

Reviewing Education and the Arts Project (REAP), Project Zero. www.pz.harvard.edu/Research/REAP.htm

SUAVE, California State University, San Marcos, 333 S. Twin Oaks Valley Rd., San Marcos, CA 92096-0001; 760-750-4000. ww2.csusm.edu/SUAVE

Preserving Kindergarten in a High-Stakes Environment

By Karen Kelly

Bonnie Walmsley remembers the kindergartners who arrived at her classroom 14 years ago. For most, it was their first experience of school. Some knew the alphabet and could count to ten. The rare student could read or write.

Today, Walmsley encounters a much wider range of abilities. Many children come in with more sophisticated skills, which she attributes partly to greater exposure to television and computers. Most have attended daycare programs. Some are 6-year-olds held back a year by parents who feared they were not mature enough for school. They share the kindergarten classroom with another population of children—5-year-olds who are still struggling to learn the alphabet and come from homes where literacy is not a priority.

"The gap has widened. There is a greater range of developmental levels now," says Walmsley, as she surveys her bustling classroom in suburban Clifton Park, N.Y. "I have one child who is doing multiplication and another who's still trying to identify numbers. It's become more challenging as a teacher."

At the same time, teachers in the older grades are facing the pressure of new standards. If their students are going to succeed on standardized tests, these teachers argue, they need to learn more before they get here—and that often means higher expectations for kindergartners. Many educators fear this is turning kindergarten into a pressure cooker, in which youngsters who can't keep up will be left behind. In Walmsley's words, "This is what 1st grade used to be."

FIGHTING THE TREND

But teachers like Walmsley and organizations like the National Association for the Education of Young Children (NAEYC) are fighting this trend. They insist that the fundamental goals of kindergarten must remain the same: helping each child develop emotionally and socially, as well as academically. Good kindergarten teachers, they maintain, are ready to teach children at every level.

"The expectations for kindergarten have gone up dramatically," says Sean Walmsley, a reading professor at the State University of New York at Albany who has written several books on kindergarten with his wife Bonnie. "It's partly the result of the states raising standards in the older grades. They've started saying, 'We've got to get kids further along,' and that means starting earlier."

Deborah Meier says these changes have been detrimental to kindergartners. Meier is co-principal of the Mission Hill School in Boston, a school modeled after the creative, open-ended learning style she instituted at the Central Park East Schools in New York City. As someone who works to extend the exploratory kindergarten experience into later grades, she is discouraged by the changes in the kindergarten classroom. "It's become an imitation of someone's idea of what 1st and 2nd grade should be," she says. "It's become more skill-driven; there's more direct instruction and less play. I think it's unequivocally bad."

Some teachers, like Jane F. Walsh of the Bowen School in Newton Center, Mass., take the increased pressure with a grain of salt. "Outside influences have an effect," admits Walsh, who has heard concerns from 4th-grade teachers preparing for the state's standardized test, "but there are always some fundamental things that will remain the same. While adult needs have changed, children's needs haven't."

Walsh believes the change in the kindergarten learning environment has more to do with the better preparation of entering students than with pressure from outside. A growing number of children are coming in with previous structured learning experiences. According to the National Center for Education Statistics (NCES), the number of children entering kindergarten from formal preschool and daycare programs has increased eightfold. "Kindergarten used to be a child's first social experience," says Annmarie Rush, a consultant who accredits schools for the NAEYC. "Now, most already know how to share and take turns. Those skills, traditionally taught in kindergarten, are already intact."

But while there is no widespread evidence of change in the kindergarten curriculum, researchers like Lorrie Shepard of the University of Colorado have found indications that the pressure on kindergarten is intensifying. Shepard wrote in 1988 of a district that prescribed a certain number of minutes be spent each day on math and reading.

That increased focus on standards has led to a rise in what Shepard calls "high-stakes testing" in kindergarten—the use of assessments to retain kindergartners, or to prevent children from entering kindergarten with their agemates.

DEFINING READINESS

Ever since the National Education Goals Panel under former President Clinton established its first goal—"By the year 2000, all children in America will start school ready to learn"—educators have been struggling to define readiness. As is often the case, they have turned to testing for help. More recently, the Bush administration's No Child Left Behind legislation has brought testing even more to the forefront of educational decision-making.

In many districts in the 1980s, pre-kindergarten screening tests became the basis for deciding which children were allowed into kindergarten. The tests also determined who was sent to a transitional extra-year program or a special education program. According to the National Academy of Sciences, in 1988 pre-kindergarten tests were required in at least 16 states and were in use by districts in at least 37 states.

The problem, says Samuel Meisels of the University of Michigan, is that the tests weren't good at predicting success. "No readiness tests have yet been developed that have acceptable predictive validity," Meisels has written. "Without a reasonable level of accuracy, the probability is high that there will be false identifications, mistaken placements, and inappropriate classifications."

A 1991 study in the journal *Educational Evaluation and Policy Analysis* supported Meisels's conclusion. Researchers studied four popular readiness tests and tracked children in nine Virginia school districts from kindergarten through 1st grade. They found that three of the four tests were fairly reliable in measuring a child's skills, but none was a good predictor of how students would perform the following year.

Bonnie Walmsley uses portfolios to track the progress of her kindergartners. Each portfolio contains samples of a student's work in writing and mathematics. The predictive value of portfolio assessments at this age hasn't been proven either. But Walmsley doesn't use them to make high-stakes decisions about her students; she simply relies on them to inform her and other teachers about children's progress.

Gilbert Gredler of the University of South Carolina believes that such assessments are more appropriate than high-stakes tests, but that when it comes to predicting a kindergartner's future performance, neither tests nor teachers are very reliable: "It's not the fault of the test. You're dealing with a very fluid group of children who are developmentally changing at a rapid rate, so it's difficult to predict their future success."

In fact, according to "Principles and Recommendations for Early Childhood Assessments," a 1998 study conducted for the National Education Goals Panel, there is a high margin of error in any assessment of a child before age eight: "Young children learn in ways and at rates different from older children. Because young children develop and learn so fast, tests given at one point in time may not give a complete picture of learning. And because young children's achievements at any point are the result of a complex mix of their ability to learn and past learning opportunities, it is a mistake to interpret measures of past learning as evidence of what could be learned."

EXTRA-YEAR PROGRAMS

Even with the increased influence of preschools and computers, there are always kindergartners who seem a little behind. They can't tie their shoes, sit still, or recite the letters of the alphabet, and they often don't perform well on kindergarten screening tests. Many educators and parents argue that these children need an extra year in a program to mature. While this is a widely used tactic, the research suggests that these programs are not effective.

For instance, a statewide study done for the Virginia Department of Education found no advantage to an extra year either before or after kindergarten for 5- or 6-year-olds. In some studies, extra-year children lagged behind their promoted peers in academic, behavioral, and visual-motor measures at the end of their additional year. Lorrie Shepard, who reviewed the research on this topic, also found no evidence that extra-year programs are effective.

But teachers like Cindy Wilson of Madill Elementary School in Ogdensburg, N.Y., believe there is a place for transitional programs. This year, three of Wilson's 23 kindergartners spent an extra year in a developmental kindergarten program. "In this area, many children haven't been to nursery school or Head Start. This is their first exposure to school. . . . We work with them on those basics." Wilson adds that the extra-year program has eliminated the use of kindergarten retention.

RETENTION

While extra-year programs have not proven effective, several studies suggest that retaining young children may actually be harmful. According to the NCES, more than 5 percent of kindergartners are retained each year. In 1997, NCES researchers interviewed the parents of more than 7,000 over-age children in 1st and 2nd grade—some who had entered kindergarten late and others who had been retained. They found that retained children were more likely to struggle academically in the later grades. This study echoes a large body of research that has found retention to be associated with lower achievement, poor attendance, and poor attitudes toward school.

Another common practice is holding a child out of kindergarten an extra year. An estimated 3 to 4 percent of kindergartners wait a year to start school because their parents feel they need more time to mature.

In its study, the NCES found mixed results of delayed entry. Students who had been held out of kindergarten were less likely than other children to receive negative feedback from their teachers concerning academic performance or behavior and less likely to be retained in later grades. But sitting out a year did not have a significant effect on their school performance.

A KINDERGARTEN FOR EVERYONE

"The hunters are out hunting for turkey today."
"My pt [party]."

Both these sentences were written by 5-year-olds in Bonnie Walmsley's kindergarten class. The first has perfect spelling and punctuation. The second is barely readable. But Walmsley says both students belong in her classroom. "A lot of it has to do with their family background. The kids who come from literate families aren't necessarily brighter; they're just further along in their learning." As for the students from less literate families, she says, "I have to plug into where they are and move them along. It's amazing how quickly they pick it up. They're bright, but they haven't all had the same experiences."

The 22 students in Walmsley's classroom are rarely engaged in the same activity at the same time. They work in twos and threes at stations or "learning centers" around the room. There's a math center, with jars filled with things like buttons, plastic dinosaurs, and colorful pompons. Walmsley helps one girl start a pattern with red, blue, and green poker chips and then asks her which color comes next. The girl adds a red one and continues the pattern.

Walmsley says activities like these allow children to work up to their own ability: "A lot of teachers would rather have them all working on the same worksheet. But then you're losing some and not challenging others. I try to push them individually as far they can go."

This approach reflects the "developmentally appropriate" practices called for by the NAEYC. The group has taken a leading role in advocating for a kindergarten that caters to all students, not just those from educationally rich backgrounds. "A developmentally appropriate curriculum responds to the needs of the age group you're teaching and the individual children within that. It provides them with everyday, concrete experiences to help them learn," explains Annmarie Rush. "So it's hands-on learning, rather than worksheets. This fosters their learning, growth, and development and provides them with the critical thinking skills they'll need in later grades."

Carmen Farina adopted this approach when she became principal of Public School 6 in New York City. She eliminated the tracking system and raised the expectations for all children, not just those in the gifted program. The school is now ranked third in the city in reading proficiency.

Like Walmsley, Farina uses learning centers in her kindergarten classrooms. Rather than placing a primary emphasis on testing to determine what students know, Farina believes in working with each child at the child's own level and progressing from there. She says there is no better place to do that than in kindergarten: "Kindergarten is the most teachable of moments. You take the children when they come to school and move them as far as they're ready to go. It's not a pressure cooker—it's about stimulating kids and keeping them energized so they want to learn more and more."

This chapter originally appeared in the Harvard Education Letter's *May/June 1999 issue. It appears primarily in its original form, although minor changes have been made for this volume.*

FOR FURTHER INFORMATION

S. Bredekamp and C. Copple, eds. *Developmentally Appropriate Practice in Early Childhood Programs Serving Children from Birth through Age 8*, rev. ed. Washington, D.C.: National Association for the Education of Young Children, 1997.

S.J. Meisels. "Doing Harm by Doing Good: Iatrogenic Effects of Early Childhood Enrollment and Promotion Policies." *Early Childhood Research Quarterly* 7 (1992): 155–174.

S.J. Meisels. "Assessing Readiness." In R.C. Pianta and M.M. Cox, eds. *The Transition to Kindergarten*. Baltimore: Paul H. Brookes, 1999.

L. Shepard, S.L. Kagan, and E. Wurtz, eds. *Principles and Recommendations for Early Childhood Assessments*. Washington, D.C.: National Education Goals Panel, 1998.

B. Walmsley, A.M. Camp, and S.A. Walmsley. *Teaching Kindergarten: A Developmentally Appropriate Approach*. Portsmouth, N.H.: Heinemann, 1992.

B. Walmsley and S.A. Walmsley. *Kindergarten: Ready or Not?* Portsmouth, N.H.: Heinemann, 1996.

Appendices

Appendix A
Key Assessment and Accountability Requirements under the No Child Left Behind Act

In January 2002, President George W. Bush signed the No Child Left Behind (NCLB) Act of 2001 into law. The legislation is a far-reaching set of school reform regulations governing such things as reading instruction, school choice, and programming for English-language learners. Perhaps the most widely publicized and controversial aspects of the law require states to develop and administer annual tests and to use those tests to hold schools accountable for improving student performance. The following excerpts from the U.S. Department of Education's "No Child Left Behind: A Desktop Reference" highlight key elements of the assessment and accountability provisions of NCLB that affect states, districts, schools, and educators.

ASSESSMENTS

By the 2005–06 school year, states must develop and implement annual assessments in reading and mathematics in grades 3 through 8 and at least once in grades 10–12. By 2007–08, states also must administer annual science assessments at least once in grades 3–5, grades 6–9, and grades 10–12. These assessments must be aligned with state academic content and achievement standards and involve multiple measures, including measures of higher-order thinking and understanding.

Alignment with State Standards. State assessments must be aligned with challenging academic content standards and challenging academic achievement standards. States were required under the previous law to develop or adopt standards in mathematics and reading/language arts, and the new law requires the development of science standards by 2005 and 2006. Their standards must have the same expectations for all children and have at least three achievement levels.

Inclusion. State assessments must provide for the participation of all students, including students with disabilities or limited English proficiency. Students who have been in schools in the United States for three consecutive years must be assessed in English in the area of reading and language arts.

Accommodations. State assessments must provide for reasonable accommodations for students with disabilities or limited English proficiency, including, if practicable, native-language versions of the assessment.

Annual Assessment of English Proficiency. Beginning with the 2002–03 school year, states must ensure that districts administer tests of English proficiency—that measure oral language, reading, and writing skills in English—to all limited English proficient students.

Reporting. State assessment systems must produce results disaggregated by gender, major racial and ethnic groups, English proficiency, migrant status, disability, and status as economically advantaged. The assessment system must produce individual student interpretive, descriptive, and diagnostic reports. States must report itemized score analyses to districts and schools.

Prompt Dissemination of Results. States must ensure that the results of state assessments administered in one school year are available to school districts before the beginning of the next school year. The assessment results must be provided in a manner that is clear and easy to understand and be used by school districts, schools and teachers to improve the educational achievement of individual students.

Participation in State NAEP. States must participate in biennial National Assessment of Educational Progress (NAEP) assessments in reading and mathematics for fourth- and eighth-graders, beginning in 2002–03. State-level NAEP data will enable policymakers to examine the relative rigor of state standards and assessments against a common metric.

ACCOUNTABILITY

States must develop and implement a single, statewide accountability system that will be effective in ensuring that all districts and schools make adequate yearly progress, and hold accountable those that do not. Schools that do not make adequate yearly progress will be identified for increasingly rigorous sanctions designed to bring about meaningful change in instruction and performance. Further, students in low-performing schools will have the option to transfer to other public schools or to obtain supplemental educational services. Finally, the law mandates the fundamental restructuring of any school that fails to improve over an extended period of time.

Adequate Yearly Progress. States must establish a definition of adequate yearly progress that each district and school is expected to meet. States must specify annual objectives to measure progress of schools and districts to ensure that all groups of students—including low-income students, students from major racial and ethnic groups, students with disabilities, and students with limited English proficiency—reach proficiency within 12 years. States must set intermediate goals that provide for annual adequate yearly progress targets, with the first increase to occur no later than 2004–05. In order to make adequate yearly progress, schools must test at least 95 percent of their students in each of the above groups.

Identification of Schools and Districts in Need of Improvement. States must annually review the progress of each school and school district receiving Title I funds to determine whether they are making adequate yearly progress, and then publicize and disseminate the results of the review. Title I schools and districts that fail to make adequate yearly progress for two consecutive years must be identified as in need of improvement.

Public School Choice. Students in schools identified for improvement must be given the option to transfer to another public school that has not been identified for improvement, with transportation provided as described below.

Professional development. Schools identified for improvement must spend at least 10 percent of their Title I Part A funds on professional development for the school's teachers and principal that directly addresses the academic achievement problem that caused the school to be identified for improvement.

Supplemental Educational Services. If a school fails to make adequate yearly progress for a third year, students from low-income families in the school must be given the option to use Title I funds to obtain supplemental educational services from a public- or private-sector provider, including faith-based organizations, selected from a list of providers approved by the state.

States must develop and apply objective criteria to potential providers that are based on a demonstrated record of effectiveness in increasing academic proficiency, and must monitor the quality and effectiveness of the services offered by approved providers. States must maintain a list of approved providers across the state, by school district, from which parents may select, and must promote maximum participation by supplemental educational services providers to ensure that parents have as many choices as possible.

Funds for Transportation and Supplemental Services. School districts are required to spend an amount equal to 20 percent of their Title I, Part A, funds to pay for supplemental educational services for eligible students and for transportation of students exercising the public school choice option, unless a lesser amount is needed to meet all requests. These funds do not have to be taken from Title I allocations, but may be provided from other allowable federal, state, local, or private sources, including federal funds under Section 1003, Title V, Part A; Title II, Part A; Title II, Part D; Title IV, Part A; and Title V, Part A (in some cases, these funds may only be used for this purpose under the transferability provision described below).

Corrective Action. If a **school** fails to make adequate yearly progress for a fourth year, the school district must take corrective actions that are designed to bring about meaningful change at the school. These corrective actions must include at least one of the following: replacing school staff, implementing a new curriculum (with appropriate professional development), decreasing management authority at the school level, appointing an outside expert to advise the school, extending the school day or year or reorganizing the school internally.

Similarly, if a **school district** fails to make adequate yearly progress for four years, the state must take corrective actions that must include at least one of the following: deferring programmatic funds or reducing administrative funds; implementing a new curriculum (with professional development); replacing personnel; establishing alternative governance arrangements; appointing a receiver or trustee to administer the district in place of the superintendent and school board; or abolishing or restructuring the school district. The state may also authorize students to transfer to higher-performing public schools operated by another school district (with transportation). States must provide information to parents and the public on any corrective action the state takes with school districts.

Restructuring. If a school fails to make adequate yearly progress for a fifth year, the school district must initiate plans to fundamentally restructure the school. This restructuring may include reopening the school as a charter school, replacing all or most of the school staff who are relevant to the failure to make adequate progress, or turning over school operations either to the state or to a private company with a demonstrated record of effectiveness.

Technical Assistance. States and school districts must provide technical assistance to schools identified for school improvement, corrective action, or restructuring. States are required to reserve portions of their Title I funding to benefit schools identified for school improvement, corrective action, and restructuring, and they must distribute 95 percent of these reserved funds to school districts. State assistance must include: establishing school support teams; designating and using distinguished teachers and principals who are chosen from schools that have been especially successful in improving academic achievement; and devising additional approaches to providing assistance, such as through institutions of higher education and educational service agencies or other local consortia, and private providers of scientifically based technical assistance.

State Report Cards. States must produce and disseminate annual report cards that provide information on how students are achieving overall as well as information disaggregated by race, ethnicity, gender,

English proficiency, migrant status, disability status, and low-income status. The report cards must include:

- State assessment results by performance level, showing two-year trend data for each subject and grade tested, with a comparison between annual objectives and actual performance for each student group. The report cards also must show the percentage of each group of students not tested.
- Graduation rates for secondary school students and any other student achievement indicators that the state chooses.
- Performance of school districts on adequate yearly progress measures, including the number and names of schools identified as in need of improvement.
- Professional qualifications of teachers in the state, including the percentage of teachers teaching with emergency or provisional credentials and the percentage of classes in the state that are not taught by highly qualified teachers, including a comparison between high- and low-poverty schools.

School District Report Cards. School districts also must prepare and disseminate annual report cards that include information on student achievement for the district and for each school. As with the state report cards, achievement data must be disaggregated for the same student subgroups. The report cards also must provide information on the schools identified for improvement.

Annual State Report to the Secretary. States must report annually to the secretary of Education on their progress in developing and implementing academic assessments; students' achievement on the assessments disaggregated by groups of students; and information about acquisition of English proficiency by children with limited English proficiency, the names of schools identified as in need of improvement, public school choice, supplemental service programs, and teacher quality.

Source: U.S. Department of Education, Office of Elementary and Secondary Education, "No Child Left Behind: A Desktop Reference." Washington, D.C., 2002.

Appendix B

What the AERA Says about High-Stakes Testing

Pressure to raise test scores can force state- and district-level officials to make decisions that may run contrary to what's best for students, education researchers say. In an effort to provide research-based guidelines to policymakers, test publishers, and school personnel, the American Educational Research Association (AERA) issued a position statement in July 2000 on the use of high-stakes testing in pre-K–12 education. According to its authors, the statement presents "a set of conditions essential to sound implementation of high-stakes testing programs." The conditions, summarized here, include:

Protection Against High-Stakes Decisions Based on a Single Test

"Decisions that affect individual students' life chances or educational opportunities should not be made on the basis of test scores alone . . ." At the very least, the AERA recommends that students be given multiple opportunities to pass high-stakes tests and that alternative forms of assessment be provided where there is "credible evidence" that a test may not measure a child's true level of proficiency.

Adequate Resources and Opportunity to Learn

Before students, schools, and districts can be "passed" or "failed" by high-stakes tests, they must have access to the materials, curriculum, and instruction to enable them to succeed on such assessments: "When content standards and associated tests are introduced as a reform to change and thereby improve current practice, opportunities to access appropriate materials and retraining consistent with the intended changes should be provided before schools, teachers, or students are sanctioned for failing to meet the new standards."

Validation for Each Separate Intended Use

Tests must only be used for the purposes for which they are valid, and each use of a particular test must be subject to "a separate evaluation of the strengths and limitations of both the testing program and the test itself."

Full Disclosure of Likely Negative Consequences

"Where credible scientific evidence suggests that a given type of testing program is likely to have negative side effects, test developers and users should make a serious effort to explain these possible effects to policymakers," recommends the AERA.

Alignment Between the Test and the Curriculum

The test should reflect the curriculum in both its content and the cognitive processes involved: "High-stakes tests should not be limited to that portion of the relevant curriculum that is easiest to measure." To avoid the problem of "teaching to the test," the AERA recommends using multiple test forms "to avoid a narrowing of the curriculum toward just the content sampled on a particular form."

Opportunities for Meaningful Remediation

Students who fail a high-stakes test should be given a second chance, and "remediation should focus on the knowledge and skills the test is intended to address, not just the test performance itself."

Additional conditions for sound testing implementation outlined in the statement include: setting valid and appropriate passing levels; taking into consideration language differences among examinees; paying appropriate attention to students with disabilities; and performing ongoing evaluations of the intended and unintended effects of high-stakes testing.

This summary originally appeared in the Harvard Education Letter's *September/ October 2000 issue. The full text of the AERA position statement is available online at www.aera.net*

About the Contributors

Lisa Birk, a former assistant editor of the *Harvard Education Letter*, is a freelance writer living in Cambridge, Mass. Her work has appeared in such publications as *Abnormal Psychology* (W. W. Norton), *Sojourner*, and the *Boston Phoenix*. She was formerly a teacher and project manager of the Nieman Program on Narrative Journalism at Harvard University.

Jane Buchbinder is the editor of the Harvard Graduate School of Education's award-winning magazine *Ed.* and a published fiction writer. She previously worked as an arts administrator for a foundation serving New England artists and organizations.

Jeff Howard is founder and president of the Efficacy Institute, Inc. He has more than 25 years' experience as a staff developer and consultant to school and community leaders on systemic education reform, and as a consultant to corporate executives and senior managers of Fortune 1000 companies in the arena of diversity and human development.

Karen Kelly is a freelance writer and public radio reporter based in Ottawa, Ontario. She reports frequently on issues related to education, the environment, and U.S.-Canada relations.

Judith A. Langer is department chair of educational theory and practice and director of the National Research Center on English Learning and Achievement (CELA) at the University at Albany, State University of New York. She has written or edited eight books and has authored numerous articles on language, literacy, and learning.

Marya R. Levenson is professor of the practice of education and Harry S. Levitan Director of Teacher Education at Brandeis University. A longtime member of the *Harvard Education Letter*'s editorial board, she has worked as a superintendent, principal, and teacher.

W. James Popham is professor emeritus at the University of California-Los Angeles Graduate School of Education and Information Studies. He has spent the bulk of his career as a teacher, first in an Oregon high school and later at UCLA, where *UCLA Today* recognized him as one of the university's top 20 professors of the 20th century. ·

Michael Sadowski is assistant editor of the *Harvard Education Letter* and the editor of *Adolescents at School: Perspectives on Youth, Identity, and Education* (Harvard Education Press, 2003). A former high school teacher, he is also an instructor and advanced doctoral candidate at the Harvard Graduate School of Education.

Rebecca Wisniewski is a Title I resource teacher who teaches reading and writing at the Charlotte M. Murkland School in Lowell, Mass. Her work with action research began with Don Bouchard at the Northeast and Islands Regional Educational Laboratory (LAB) at Brown University.